PRIZES, GRANTS AND BURSARIES 1998.

A DETAILED GUIDE TO OVER

£1 MILLION IN AWARDS FOR WRITERS

© Writers Bookshop 1997
ISBN 0 9529119 4 9

First published by Writers' Bookshop, 7-11 Kensington High Street, London, W8 5NP.

All rights reserved
Edited by Kevin Brown

A Note From The Publisher

This is a guide to 'Prizes, Grants and Bursaries', which we hope will be an invaluable tool for all writers.

The information has been supplied by the administrators themselves and is published at face value.

Where full information has not been supplied to us prior to publication we have listed the addresses after the main listings, at the back of the book.

This guide will be updated annually. If you feel we have omitted valuable information or that the guide could be improved, we would like to hear from you.

Thank you

INTRODUCTION

MARK RAINEY

Literary prizes are news!

People love to hear about writers' awards: newspapers, radio and television regularly feature the winners. Whether large national and international competitions attracting the up-and-coming literary 'names', or lesser-known local/specialist competitions receiving entries from professional and casual writers alike, all attract media publicity.

How is the writer to know about the competition *before* the winner is announced, so that they, too, can enter? Writers' Bookshop has the solution: a comprehensive listing and description of literary competitions across the nation. It is the most comprehensive guide of its kind.

There is no short cut to winning, but being ahead of the game helps. Entries are clearly and simply laid out, so you can easily choose the competition most suited to your style of writing - and give yourself the best chance of success.

Should you win, the boost and encouragement will be invaluable, of course: but this is not the only reason to enter. Enter for the fun of it; and remember, even if you don't take the prize this time, your work will have gained exposure and been read by more people. If you are like me, this is the reason you are writing in the first place.

Good luck!

1998 Poetry Competition

Administrator	Wells Festival of Literature
Address	Wells Tourist Centre, Town Hall, Wells, Somerset BA5 1SE
Phone number	01749 672552
E.mail	

Entry fee £2 per poem

Description

Poems may be on any subject. They should be limited to not more than 40 lines.

Poems must be in English, previously unpublished, not accepted for any future publication, and not previously awarded any prize in this or any other competition.

Poems should be typed, but will be acceptable if neatly hand-written. They cannot be returned.

Each poem must be on a separate sheet, which must not bear the name or the address of the author. The author's name and address with entry fee(s) should be in a sealed envelope attached to the entry, with the title of the poem(s) written on the outside. Entries must be clearly marked Wells Festival Poetry Competition.

Frequency	Annually
Closing date	20th Sept
Payment	1st Prize £125 and publication in Outposts

Age Concern England

Administrator	Vinnette Marshall
Address	1268 London Road, London SW16 4ER
Phone number	0181 679 8000
Fax number	0181 679 6069
E.mail	books@ace.org.uk

Entry fee

Description

The Seebohm Trophy - Age Concern Book of the Year.

Entry criteria: The award will be made to the author and publisher of the non-fiction title published in the previous calendar year which, in the opinion of the judges, is most successful in promoting the well-being and understanding of older people. The winning author will receive a cheque for £1,000. The winning publisher will be presented with the silver Seebohm Trophy.

Frequency	Annually
Closing date	Early May
Payment	£1,000

Agnes Mure Mackenzie Award, The

Administrator	Mrs Kathleen Munro
Address	Saltire Society, 9 Fountain Close, 22 High Street, Edinburgh, EH1 1TF
Phone number	0131 556 1836
Fax number	0131 557 1675
E.mail	

Entry fee

Description
Established 1965, the Award - a bound and inscribed copy of the winning publication - was instituted in memory of the late Dr Agnes Mure Mackenzie, and is made biennially for a published work of Scottish Historical Research (including intellectual history and the history of science). Editions of texts are not eligible. The Award is open to books published during the calendar years 1995-96. Nominations are invited and should be sent to the Administrator.

Frequency	Biennially
Closing date	
Payment	

Aileen & Albert Sanders Memorial Trophy

Administrator	Ivan Sanders
Address	13 Milton Crescent, Leicester, LE4 0PA
Phone number	
Fax number	
E.mail	
Entry fee	£3 single, £5 for two poems

Description

The competition will be open as to subject, form and style, except that poems must be in English or Scots and not exceed 40 lines.

Only UK residents will be eligible for the winner's trophy which must be returned at least one month prior to the closing date for next year's competition.

Each poem must be typed on a separate sheet, and must not bear the author's details. The author's details, together with a list of poems submitted should be provided on a separate sheet. No entry form required. Poems will not be returned. For results enclose sae marked 'Results'.

Poems must be unpublished and not have previously won a prize. No alterations my be made to entered poems. Winners consent to their names and address being released, but not telephone numbers.

Frequency	Annually
Closing date	January
Payment	£500 + Trophy

Alexander Prize, The

Administrator	University College London
Address	Gower Street, London WC1E 6BT
Phone number	0171 387 7532
Fax number	0171 387 7532

Description

The Alexander Prize is offered annually for a paper based on original historical research. The winner of the prize is awarded £250.

The prize provides an opportunity for historians to gain both national recognition and guaranteed publication of their work.

Candidates must either be under the age of 35 or be registered for a higher degree or have been registered for such a degree within the last three years.

The paper will be read to a meeting of the Royal Historical Society and will then be published in the Society's Transactions.

The paper - which must not exceed 8,000 words including footnotes - can relate to any historical subject approved by a Literary Director of the Society.

The paper may be derived from a doctoral thesis (either in progress or completed), but it should be self-contained and suitable for reading as a lecture.

Entry forms are available from the Executive Secretary.

Frequency	Annually
Closing date	
Payment	£250

Alfred Bradley Bursary Award

Administrator	Melanie Harris
Address	BBC Radio Drama, New Broadcasting House, Oxford Road, Manchester M60 1SJ
Phone number	0161 244 4254
Fax number	0161 244 4248
E.mail	mharris@radio.mr.bbc

Entry fee

Description

Founded in 1912, this biennial bursary of up to £6,000 spread over two years together with a full commission for a radio play, is awarded to one or several writers resident or born in the North of England who have had a small amount of work published or produced. Writers will be invited to submit a new radio play for the 1998-99 award in February 1998.

Frequency	Biennially
Closing date	May
Payment	£6,000

Allied Domecq Playwright And Translation Awards, The

Administrator	Allied Domecq Plc
Address	Tower House, 8-14 Southampton Street, Covent Garden, London, WC2E 7HA
Phone number	0171 379 3234
Fax number	0171 465 8241
E.mail	

Entry fee

Description

Allied Domecq Plc, the leading international drinks and retailing company, and principal sponsor of the RSC, has teamed up with the Arts Council, the Bush Theatre and the Gate Theatre, to offer playwrights and translators of all ages (above 18) and backgrounds the opportunity to apply for a £5000 award. The successful writer/translator will not only receive financial support (to help with the writing/translating of the play) but will have the chance of having the play produced and staged at the Bush/Gate. Allied Domecq Plc want to maintain its long-standing relationship with fringe theatre and unearth new talent.

Frequency	Biennially
Closing date	Early January
Payment	£5,000

Annual LACE Open Poetry Competition, The

Administrator   The Secretary

Address   The Day Centre, Park Street, Lincoln, Lincs
                      LN1 1UQ

Phone number

Fax number

E.mail

Entry fee   £4 per poem

Description

Poems may be in any subject, but no longer than 40 lines.

Poems must not have won an award in any other competition, not have been published or submitted elsewhere.

Any number of poems may be entered.

Enter your full name and address on the Entry Form, together with the titles of the poems.

Note: Your name must not appear on any poem sheet.

Entries only accepted from the United Kingdom and Northern Ireland.

Note: Stamped addressed envelopes are required for acknowledgement of entry and also for list of prizewinners.

Frequency   Annually

Payment   £80

Apple Tree Award

Administrator	Reach! National Resource Centre for Children with Reading Difficulties
Address	Wellington House, Wellington Road, Wokingham, Berkshire RG40 2AG
Phone number	0118 989 1101
Fax number	0118 979 0989
E.mail	reach@reach-reading.demon.co.uk
Entry fee	None

Description

An award for creative writing by children who have difficulty with reading, writing and communication. The award alternates between poetry and prose. There are four age groups covering junior and secondary schools. Entries may be submitted in handwriting, typed script, computer produced, Braille (with transcription), signed video (with transcription), Rebus or Bliss (with transcription). One prize-winner in each section.

Prize: A hand-carved apple and a book token.

Some Highly Commended certificates are awarded.

All entrants receive a certificate. Judges include a writer and a language consultant.

Frequency	Annual
Closing date	Easter
Payment	£200 Prize Fund

Arts Council Of England

Administrator   Chairman -Mr Gerry Robinson

Address   14 Great Peter Street, London SW1P 3NQ

Phone number   0171 333 0100

Fax number   0171 973 6590

E.mail

Entry fee

Description
The Arts Council Of England receives public money from the Government to support and develop the Arts in England. From this the Arts Council provides regular funding to Arts organisations, as well as one-off grants - 'Development Funds'. In addition the Arts Council is one of the distributors of National Lottery Funds to the Arts. Contact the Arts Council for further information on the Development Funds and the Lottery Funding Programmes.

Frequency

Closing date

Payment

Arts Council Of Wales Book Of The Year Awards, The

Administrator	The Arts Council Of Wales
Address	9 Museum Place, Cardiff, CF1 3NX
Phone number	01222 394711
Fax number	01222 221447
E.mail	
Entry fee	None

Description

The Arts Council of Wales Book of the Year Awards are given annually for works of exceptional merit by Welsh authors (by birth or residence) published during the previous calendar year. Works may be in Welsh or English. Two prizes of £3,000 are awarded to the winners and £1,000 to four other shortlisted authors in the categories of poetry, fiction and creative non-fiction, including literary criticism, biography and autobiography. In the case of non-fiction, the subject-matter must be concerned with Wales.

Frequency	Annually
Closing date	31st December
Payment	£10,000 Prize Fund

Authors' Club First Novel Award

Administrator	Authors' Club
Address	40 Dover Street, London W1X 3RB
Phone number	0171 499 8581
Fax number	0171 409 0913
E.mail	

Entry fee

Description
Contact Mrs Ann Carter

Established 1954. This award is made for the most promising work published in Britain by a British author, and is presented at a dinner held at the Authors' Club. Entries for the award are accepted from publishers and must be full-length - short stories are not eligible.

Frequency

Closing date

Payment   £750

Authors' Contingency Fund, The

Administrator	The Society Of Authors
Address	84 Drayton Gardens, London, SW10 9SB
Phone number	0171 373 6642
Fax number	0171 373 5768
E.mail	authorsoc@writers.org.uk

Entry fee

Description
A number of emergency grants are made each year to professional authors who are in immediate financial difficulties or for the financial relief of their dependants.

Write for an application form

Frequency

Closing date

Payment

Authors' Foundation, The

Administrator	The Society Of Authors
Address	84 Drayton Gardens, London, SW10 9SB
Phone number	0171 373 6642
Fax number	0171 373 5768
E.mail	authorsoc@writers.org.uk

Description

Eligibility:

1. Any author who has been commissioned by a British publisher to write a full-length work of fiction, poetry or non-fiction and who needs funding (in addition to the publisher's advance) for important research, travel, or other more general expenditure may apply.

2. Without a contractual commitment by a publisher you may apply so long as you have had a book published and there is a strong likelihood that your next book will be published.

How to apply:

Application is made by letter (2-3 pages), including the following:

1. brief information about yourself and your books, including details of the book on which you are working;

2. an explanation of your financial position (including details of the publisher's advance) and preferably specifying the sum needed, with reasons (bearing in mind that even the largest grants are unlikely to exceed £5,000);

3. enclose a few reviews of your work, if available (not more than 3-4 pages on A4 paper - and not original newspaper cuttings).

Closing date   April
Payment £5,000 maximum

Benson Medal

Administrator	Mrs Maggie Fergusson
Address	The Royal Society of Literature, 1 Hyde Park Gardens, London, W2 2LT
Phone number	0171 723 5104
Fax number	0171 402 0199
E.mail	

Entry fee

Description
Benson Medal: Founded in 1916 by A C Benson, distinguished scholar, writer and Fellow of the Society, in respect of meritorious works 'in poetry, fiction, history, biography and belles lettres'. It is awarded irregularly and is now regarded as the crown of a career rather than a recognition of a single work. Since its inception it has been awarded 35 times, most recently to Julien Green.

The medal is 2 3/4" in diameter and is solid silver. It bears the recipient's name on one side, and on the reverse, the head of George IV, the Society's founder, with the inscription GEORGIUS IV REG: SOC: LIT: FUNDATOR ET PATRONUS MDCCCXXIII.

Frequency	Irregular
Closing date	
Payment	

Betty Trask Award, The

Administrator	The Society of Authors
Address	84 Drayton Gardens, London SW10 9SB
Phone number	0171 373 6642
Fax number	0171 373 5768
E.mail	authorsoc@writers.org.uk

Description

The Betty Trask Awards are for the benefit of young authors (under 35) and are given on the strength of a first novel (published or unpublished) of a romantic or traditional nature. In 1998, there will be at least £25,000 available for a Betty Trask Prize (which may be divided) and up to five additional Betty Trask Awards. The winners are required to use the money for foreign travel.

Unpublished works: two copies of a typescript (both easily legible and showing the author's name as well as any pseudonym) should be submitted. Typescripts will be returned only if the author provides a stamped, self addressed package.

Please also send a stamped, self-addressed envelope for us to acknowledge their receipt.

Neither the judges nor the Society of Authors can take responsibility for typescripts, which are sent at the author's risk. Authors are strongly advised to keep a spare copy.

First published novels and unpublished novels at proof stage: six copies (non-returnable) should be submitted by the publishers.

Frequency	Annually
Closing date	31st January
Payment	£25,000

Bigot Of The Year

Administrator	Anny Bracky
Address	Granta House, 15-19 Broadway, London. E15 4BQ
Phone number	0181 519 2122
Fax number	0181 522 1725
E.mail	

Entry fee

Description
Bigot of the Year is awarded to the journalist who has stood out in terms of crass stereotyping

Frequency	Annually
Closing date	
Payment	

Boardman Tasker Prize For Mountain Literature

Administrator	Mrs Dorothy Boardman
Address	14 Pine Lodge, Dairyground Road, Bramhall, Stockport, SK7 2HS
Phone number	0161 439 4624

Entry fee

Description

The prize of £2000 commemorates the lives of Peter Boardman and Joe Tasker and is given to the author of an original work which has made an outstanding contribution to mountain literature.

Books with a mountain, not necessarily a mountaineering theme, whether fiction, non-fiction, drama or poetry, written in the English language (initially or in translation) are eligible.

Entry, in book format, and not the format of a magazine, periodical or anthology, is by publishers only.

Confined to books published between 1st November of the previous year and 31st October of the year of the prize.

Apply to administrator for entry forms.

Frequency	Annually
Closing date	1st August
Payment	£2,000

Book & Pamphlet Competition

Administrator	The Poetry Business
Address	The Studio, Byram Arcade, Westgate, Huddersfield HD1 1ND
Phone number	01484 434840
Fax number	01484 426566
E.mail	poetry-business@geo2.poptel.org.uk
Entry fee	£15

Description
Send a small collection of poems (16-24 pages). Choose a pen name and title for the collection then send it with an entry form.

Frequency	Annually
Closing date	October
Payment	£1,000 Prize Fund

Booker Prize For Fiction

Administrator	Book Trust
Address	Book House, 45 East Hill, London SW18 2QZ
Phone number	0181 870 9055
Fax number	0181 874 4790
E.mail	

Entry fee

Description
Awarded to the best full-length novel of the year. Entrants must be UK citizens, Republic of Ireland or Commonwealth citizens. The book must have been published in the UK between 1st October and the following 30th September.

Frequency	Annually
Closing date	31st July
Payment	£20,000

BP Natural World Book Prize

Administrator	Book Trust
Address	Book House, 45 East Hill, London SW18 2QZ
Phone number	0181 870 9055
Fax number	0181 874 4790
E.mail	

Entry fee

Description
Awarded to a book that most imaginatively promotes the understanding and conservation of the natural environment. Entries must be published during the calendar year of the award.

Frequency	Annually
Closing date	Contact Book Trust for details
Payment	£5,000

Bridport Prize, The

Administrator	The Competition Secretary
Address	The Arts Centre, South Street, Bridport, Dorset, DT6 3NR
Phone number	01308 427183
Fax number	01308 424204
E.mail	
Entry fee	£4.00 per item

Description

A creative writing competition for poems of not more than forty-two lines and stories of not more than five thousand words. First place £2500, second prize £1000, third prize £500 in each category, plus supplementary prizes. The three winning stories are submitted to a leading London literary agent, and an anthology of prize winning entries is published every year by the Redcliffe Press. For entry form and full details send sae to the Competition Secretary

Frequency	Annually
Closing date	30th June
Payment	£2,500

British Centre For Literary Translation Competition, The

Administrator	British Centre for Literary Translation.
Address	School of Modern Languages & European Studies, University of East Anglia, Norwich, Norfolk, NR4 7TJ
Phone number	01603 592785
Fax number	01603 592785
E.mail	c.c.wilson@uea.ac.uk
Entry fee	£5

Description

Literary and scholarly translators from the 15 European Union countries, Norway, Iceland and Liechtenstein, may apply for BCLT one-month residential bursaries on the University of East Anglian campus. They should offer the translation of a high quality 20th century literary work (novels, short stories, essays, literary histories, biographies, drama or poetry) which is representative of the culture that produced it, illustrates trends in contemporary European literature in the second half of the century, and is likely to interest a wide European public. A publisher's contract is preferred. Languages should be those of the European Union in or out of English, and may include e.g. Catalan, Basque, Welsh, Gaelic. The bursary consists of self-contained accommodation on the University of East Anglian campus, reimbursement of travel from home to Norwich, and a small cost-of-living allowance.

Frequency	Annually
Closing date	28th February
Payment	

British Fantasy Society Awards, The

Administrator   Fantasylon

Address   2 Harwood Street, Stockport, Cheshire,
                       SK4 1JJ

Phone number

Fax number

E.mail   debbie@djb.il-net.com

Entry fee

Description
The BFS Awards are voted on by the members of the society according to what they have enjoyed reading during the past year

Frequency   Annually

Closing date   Usually around April.

Payment

C B Oldman Prize

Administrator	Aberdeen University Library
Address	Queen Mother Library, Meston Walk, Aberdeen, Grampian, AB24 3UE
Phone number	01224 272592
Fax number	01224 487048
E.mail	r.turbet@abdn.ac.uk
Entry fee	None

Description
Awarded by the UK branch of the 'International Association of Music Libraries' for the best book of music bibliography, music librarianship or music reference written by an author domiciled in the U.K.

Frequency	Annually
Closing date	31st December
Payment	

Cardiff International Poetry Competition

Administrator	M Harlin
Address	Welsh Academy, 3rd Floor Mount Stuart House, Mount Stuart Square, Cardiff CF1 6DQ
Phone number	01222 492 025
Fax number	01222 492 930
E.mail	dafr@celtic.co.uk
Entry fee	£4

Description

There is, £5,000 in prizes, 1st £1,000, 2nd £750, 3rd £500 and eleven prizes of £250. Each poem must be no more than 50 lines in length and in English. For an entry form please send an SAE to: Cardiff International Poetry Competition, PO Box 438, Cardiff CF1 6YA.

Frequency	Annually
Closing date	31st October 1997
Payment	1st - £1,000

Children's Book Award, The

Administrator	Marianne Adey
Address	The Old Malt House, Aldbourne, Marlborough, Wilts, SN8 2DW
Phone number	01672 540629
Fax number	01672 541280
E.mail	106311.1205@compuserve.com

Entry fee

Description

The Children's Book Award is an annual prize for the best work of fiction for children, awarded by The Federation of Children's Book Groups. The Award, judged by children, is awarded in three categories: picture books, shorter novels and longer novels. For further information send a s.a.e. to the co-ordinator.

Frequency	Annually
Closing date	31st December
Payment	Portfolio of children's work, silver and wooden trophy

Cholmondeley Awards For Poets, The

Administrator	The Society Of Authors
Address	84 Drayton Gardens, London, SW10 9SB
Phone number	0171 373 6642
Fax number	0171 373 5768
E.mail	authorsoc@writers.org.uk

Entry fee

Description
The Cholmondeley Awards for Poets were founded by the late Dowager Marchioness of Cholmondeley in 1966 to recognise the achievement and distinction of individual poets. It is not a competitive award and submissions are not required. The recipients are chosen by the Awards Committee for their general body of work and contribution to poetry.

Frequency

Closing date

Payment

Clo Iar-Chonnachta Literary Award, The

Administrator	Clo Iar-Chonnachta
Address	Indreabhan, Co. na Gaillimhe, Eire
Phone number	+ 353 91 593307
Fax number	+ 353 91 593362
E.mail	cir@iol.ie
Entry fee	Ir £20

Description
£5,000 will be presented for a newly written and unpublished work in the Irish language. The award will be presented for the best short story collection or drama each year.

Frequency	Annually
Closing date	1st December
Payment	£5,000

Crompton Bequest, The

Administrator	The Society of Authors
Address	84 Drayton Gardens, London, SW10 9SB
Phone number	0171 373 6642
Fax number	0171 373 5768
E.mail	authorsoc@writers.org.uk

Entry fee

Description

This Bequest exists to assist the publication of works of scholarship and imagination, and takes the form of a subsidy to the publisher. The procedure is that the publisher applies to the Society of Authors, giving details of the book, and attaching a reader's report, also indicating the size of the subsidy requested.

Frequency

Closing date

Payment

David Higham Prize For Fiction

Administrator	Book Trust
Address	Book House, 45 East Hill, London SW18 2QZ
Phone number	0181 870 9055
Fax number	0181 874 4790
E.mail	

Entry fee

Description
Awarded to a first novel or book of short stories published in the calendar year of the prize.

Frequency	Annually
Closing date	31st August
Payment	£1,000

David T K Wong Fellowship In Creative Writing

Administrator	School of English and American Studies.
Address	University of East Anglia, Norwich, Norfolk, NR4 7TJ
Phone number	01603 592810
Fax number	01603 507728
E.mail	vstriker@uea.ac.uk
Entry fee	£5

Description

This newly established fellowship is a substantial annual award of £25,000, created to support writers of fiction.

The Fellow will be someone of exceptional talent who plans to write in English about life in the Far East. He or she will reside at the University of East Anglia for one year, and will be expected only to write. There are no teaching commitments.

Candidates must submit an original piece of fiction in English. Shortlisted applicants must then produce an outline of their planned writing project.

Entries will be judged on their quality and promise by a distinguished international panel, including UEA's Professor of Creative Writing, poet and biographer Andrew Motion.

Frequency	Annually
Closing date	31st October
Payment	£25,000

Dogwatch Open Poetry Competition

Administrator	Michael A Edridge
Address	267 Willbury Road, Warlingham, Surrey, CR6 9TZ
Phone number	01883 622121
Fax number	01883 622124
E.mail	
Entry fee	£2.00 first entry £1.00 subsequent entries

Description
Poems up to 40 lines - open style or theme, winning poems published in Dogwatch Newsheet (sent to all winners)

Frequency	Annually
Closing date	1st November
Payment	

Dorothy Tutin Award, The

Administrator	National Poetry Foundation
Address	27 Mill Road, Fareham, Hants PO16 0TH
Phone number	01329 822218
Fax number	01329 822218
E.mail	

Entry fee

Description
The Dorothy Tutin Award for Services to Poetry

This is an award that is 'by recommendation only' and is given to the person 'whom it is felt has done the most to encourage the writing and love of poetry in the UK'. It is only given spasmodically and we do not go out of our way to advertise it.

Frequency

Closing date

Payment

Drama Association Of Wales, The

Administrator	Kirsty Foster
Address	The Library, Singleton Road, Splott, Cardiff, CF2 2ET
Phone number	01222 452200
Fax number	01222 452277
E.mail	

Entry fee

Description

The Drama Association of Wales works in both languages of the country and puts professional advice and financial help within easy reach of every theatre-minded community in Wales. As the national body for amateur theatre, including youth theatre, DAW provides its members with a playscript lending library, drapes for hire, training courses, printing, sound effects, help in obtaining grants and total encouragement to go ahead and enjoy making theatre.

The Drama Association of Wales now holds the complete former British Theatre Association playscripts lending collection as well as a significant portion of the reference collection. DAW is now the largest specialist drama lending provision in the world!

'DAWN' the Association's magazine is published five times a year.

Frequency

Closing date

Payment

Duff Cooper Prize, The

Administrator	Ms Artemis Cooper
Address	54 Saint Maur Road, London, SW6 4DP
Phone number	0171 736 3729
Fax number	0171 731 7638
E.mail	

Entry fee

Description
The Duff Cooper Prize is awarded annually for a literary work of history or biography, published within the last year. The work must be submitted by the publisher, not the author, and the publisher must be a member of the Publisher's Association. The Prize was founded by Duff Cooper's friends, after his death in 1954. Previous prize-winners include Humphrey Carpenter, Robert Hughes, Victoria Glendinning and Hilary Spurling. The winner receives a cheque for £2,500 and a copy of Duff Cooper's autobiography, Old Men Forget.

Frequency	Annually
Closing date	31st November
Payment	£2,500

Edgar Graham Book Prize, The

Administrator	School of Oriental and African Studies.
Address	Thornhaugh Street, Russell Square, London, WC1H 0XG
Phone number	0171 691 3316
Fax number	0171 323 6605
E.mail	deustud@soas.ac.uk

Entry fee

Description

The prize is awarded every two years for a work of original scholarship on agriculture and/or industrial development in Asia and/or Africa.

This well established academic book prize of £1500 will next be awarded in 1998. Publishers are invited to submit eligible works.

The prize is open to works published in English between July 1995 and December 1997. The submission of edited books, particularly conference volumes; is not encouraged.

Frequency	Biennially
Closing date	31st March
Payment	£1,500

Eleanor Farjeon Award

Administrator	Children's Book Award.
Address	c/o Transworld Children's Books, 61-63 Uxbridge Road, London, W5 5SA
Phone number	0181 231 6648
Fax number	0181 231 6727
E.mail	

Entry fee

Description
This award named in memory of the much loved children's writer is for distinguished service to children's books either in this country or overseas, and may be given to a librarian, teacher, publisher, bookseller, author, reviewer, television producer, etc. Nominations from members of the Children's Book Circle.

Frequency	Annually
Closing date	
Payment	£750

Encore Award, The

Administrator	The Society Of Authors
Address	84 Drayton Gardens, London SW10 9SB
Phone number	0171 373 6642
Fax number	0171 373 5768
E.mail	authorsoc@writers.org.uk

Description

The Encore Award for the best second novel of the year.

Eligibility

The work submitted must be:

a) an adult novel by one author who has had one (and only one) novel published previously; and

b) in the English language, first published in the UK, and published in that year.

Judges

There will be three judges whose books may not be entered for the award. They may call in books if they so wish. The decision of the judges (both as to eligibility and the winning entries) shall be final and they reserve the right not to award the Encore Award if, in their opinion, no works entered reach a sufficiently high standard.

Frequency	Annually
Closing date	November
Payment	£7,500

Enid McLeod Literary Prize, The

Administrator	Franco-British Society
Address	Room 623, Linen Hall, 162-168 Regent Street, London W1R 5TB
Phone number	0171 734 0815
Fax number	0171 734 0815 |//
Entry fee	£18 single or £25 joint.

Description

It will be awarded annually to the author of the work of literature published in the United Kingdom which, in the opinion of the judges, has contributed most to Franco-British understanding. Only in exceptional circumstances will the prize be split between two authors.

The judges are chosen by the Council of the Franco-British Society, and the prize winner will be announced in the first three months of each year.

Eligible Books

Any full-length work of literature, written in English, by a citizen of the United Kingdom, British Commonwealth, Republic of Ireland, Pakistan, Bangladesh and South Africa, and first published in the United Kingdom, is eligible.

A book submitted on behalf of an author who has deceased at the time of publication will not be considered.

No English translation of a book written originally in any other language will be considered.

No entry shall be ineligible because its author has previously won either the Enid McLeod Literary Prize or any other prize.

Frequency	Annually
Closing date	31st December

Envoi International Poetry Competition

Administrator	Envoi
Address	44 Rudyard Road, Biddulph Moor, Stoke-on-Trent
Phone number	
Fax number	
E.mail	
Entry fee	£2 per poem, £10 for 6 poems.

Description

Unpublished poem in English - 40 lines or less.

Anonymous - name and address in accompanying ssae.

Winning poems published in Envoi with adjudicator's report.

Frequency	3 Competitions per year
Closing date	Feb 20th - June 20th - October 20th
Payment	1st Prize £100; 2nd £75; 3rd £25

Eric Gregory Trust Fund Awards, The

Administrator	The Society of Authors
Address	84 Drayton Gardens, London SW10 9SB
Phone number	0171 373 6642
Fax number	0171 373 5768
E.mail	authorsoc@writers.org.uk

Description

Candidates for awards must:

a. be British subjects by birth but not nationals of 'Eire or any of the British Dominions or Colonies', and ordinarily resident in the United Kingdom or Northern Ireland.

b. be under the age of 30 at 31 March that year.

c. submit for the consideration of the judges a published or unpublished volume of poetry, drama-poems (not more than 30), or belles-lettres.

The presentations are made annually in the summer of the year of the awards. Entries should be sent, with an accompanying letter from the candidate:

a. confirming that he or she is a British subject by birth;

b. giving his or her date of birth;

c. normal place of residence;

d. enclosing stamped self-addressed packaging for the return of the poems, and a small stamped self-addressed envelope for us to acknowledge their receipt.

Frequency	Annually
Closing date	October
Payment	£22,000

Fan Circle International

Administrator	Mrs J D Milligan
Address	Cronk-y-Voddy, 21 Rectory Road, Coltishall, Norwich, Norfolk, NR12 7HF
Phone number	01603 737270
Fax number	
E.mail	
Entry fee	£16.00 pa membership

Description

Essay Competition with subject around fans. Specific field announced with each competition.

Recently a poetry competition was tried and could be repeated.

Frequency	Biennially
Closing date	As announced in FCI's bulletin
Payment	Varies each competition

Fidler Award, The

Administrator	Book Trust Scotland
Address	Scottish Book Centre, 137 Dundee Street, Edinburgh, EH11 1BG
Phone number	0131 229 3663
Fax number	0131 228 4293
E.mail	book.trust.scotland@dial.pipex.com

Entry fee

Description

Sponsored by Hodder Children's Books, The Fidler Award is for the best first novel for children aged 8-12 years. The Fidler Award is administered by Book Trust Scotland. The winner receives a £1,000 cash prize, and the winning novel is published by Hodder Children's Books.

Frequency	Annually
Closing date	31st October
Payment	£1,000

Forward Prizes For Poetry, The

Administrator	Colman Getty PR
Address	Carrington House, 126-130 Regent Street, London W1R 5FE
Phone number	0171 439 1783
Fax number	0171 439 1784
E.mail	
Entry fee	Only Publishers or Editors can enter work for the prizes

Description

Now in its sixth year, the Forward Prizes are the UK's biggest annual awards for poetry and the only prizes which seek to reward both new and established poets. They are awarded in three categories: Best Collection of Poetry (£10,000) sponsored by Forward Publishing; Best First Collection of Poetry (£5,000) sponsored by Waterstone's; Best Single Poem (£1,000) sponsored by Tolman Cunard. They are awarded annually in October for the previous year's collections and for Single Poems, published between May and April of the previous year. An anthology of the best entries are published in the Forward Book of Poetry (Paperback £7.95) every year.

Only previously published work, published in the UK and Eire is eligible.

Frequency	Annually
Closing date	Early May
Payment	£16,000

Fraenkel Prize In Comtemporary History, The

Administrator	The Institute of Contemporary History and Wiener Library.
Address	4 Devonshire Street, London, W1N 2BH
Phone number	0171 636 7247
Fax number	0171 436 6428
E.mail	lib@wl.u-net.com

Entry fee

Description

Awarded annually by the Wiener Library, London. In 1998 two awards will be made. Both will be for an outstanding, unpublished work in one of the following fields of interest of the Wiener Library. These include the 20th Century history of Central Europe, recent Jewish history, the Second World War, fascism and totalitarianism, political violence, racism etc.

One prize of US $5,000 is open to all entrants; The length should be not less than 50,000 and not more than 150,000 words.

A second prize of US $3,000 is open to entrants who have yet to publish a major work; the length should be not less than 25,000 and not more than 100,000 words.

Candidates should specify for which of the prizes they are competing.

Applications for the 1998 prizes; two copies of the work plus a brief Curriculum Vitae should reach the Wiener Library by end April 1998.

Frequency	Annually
Closing date	End of April
Payment	$8,000

Francis Head Bequest, The

Administrator	The Society of Authors
Address	84 Drayton Gardens, London SW10 9SB
Phone number	0171 373 6642
Fax number	0171 373 5768
E.mail	authorsoc@writers.org.uk

Entry fee

Description
Mrs Head, a well-known literary agent, generously established this trust in her will with the object of making grants to professional writers (writing in the English Language) who were born in England, Scotland, Wales or Northern Ireland, and who are over the age of thirty-five. It is aimed at authors who by reasons of illness or otherwise are in financial difficulty. She particularly wished to help authors who are temporarily unable to maintain themselves or their families owing to illness or an accident, but the terms of the trust are reasonably wide.

Frequency

Closing date

Payment

Frogmore Poetry Prize, The

Administrator	The Frogmore Press
Address	42 Morehall Avenue, Folkestone, Kent, CT19 4EF
Phone number	
Fax number	
E.mail	
Entry fee	£2 per poem

Description

Founded in 1987, The Frogmore Poetry Prize has been won by a number of writers who have gone on to publish major collections: John Latham, Caroline Price, Tobias Hill, Mario Petrucci . . .

The prize is worth one hundred guineas (£105) and all shortlisted poems are published in the September issue of the bi-annual 'Frogmore Papers' (Founded 1983). Adjudication is always by an accomplished and widely published poet (John Mole, Carole Satyamurti, Linda France, Sophie Hannah, Pauline Stainer).

Frequency	Annually
Closing date	30th June
Payment	£105

Fulbright Commission, The

Administrator	The British Programme Adminstrator
Address	62 Doughty Street, London WC1N 2LS
Phone number	0171 404 6880
Fax number	0171 404 6834
E.mail	

Entry fee None

Description

The Fulbright Commission has a number of awards available annually for postgraduate study and for lecturing or research at institutions in the United States of America.

Applicants should consult the website on http.//www.fulbright.co.uk in the first instance. Otherwise requests for information should be accompanied by sae with postage for 100 grams attached.

Frequency	Annually
Closing date	
Payment	

Fulton Fellowship, The

Administrator	Barry Carpenter
Address	Centre for the Studies of Special Education, Westminster College, Oxford OX2 9AT
Phone number	01865 253319
Fax number	01865 791928
E.mail	csse@cityscape.co.uk

Entry fee None

Description

Purposes of the Fellowship

1. To support the researcher in a collaborative venture involving the Academic Institution (Westminster College) and the Publishing Company, David Fulton Publishers.

2. To strengthen the link between a research thesis and a written publication (theory into practice).

3. To disseminate research findings in a form that is accessible to educational practitioners.

4. To encourage research endeavour and scholarly activity through financial sponsorship within the area of special educational needs.

Applications

Application for the Fulton Fellowship should include:

A curriculum vitae (3 copies)

A research proposal clearly stating:

- Title of the research
- Aim of the research
- Proposed construction of the research project
- Projected outcome of the research programme in terms of a book to be published through David Fulton Publishers.

Frequency	Annually
Closing date	30th April
Payment	Equivalent to a one-year college course fee.

Gladstone Memorial Trust, The

Administrator	Royal Historical Society.
Address	University College London, Gower Street, London, WC1E 6BT
Phone number	0171 387 7532
Fax number	0171 387 7532

Entry fee

Description
The prize has been made possible by a generous grant from The Gladstone Memorial Trust and will be awarded in 1998: the centenary of Gladstone's death.

To be eligible for consideration for the prize the book must:

1. be on any historical subject which is not primarily related to British history.

2. be its authors first solely written history book;

3 have been published in English, during the calendar year 1997, by a scholar normally resident in the United Kingdom;

4 be an original and scholarly work of historical research.

Frequency

Closing date

Payment £1,000

Glenfiddich Awards, The

Administrator	Grayling P.R.
Address	4 Bedford Square, London WC1B 3RA
Phone number	0171 255 1100
Fax number	0171 631 0602
E.mail	lindsays@grayling.co.uk

Entry fee

Description

Each year The Glenfiddich Awards recognise excellence in writing, publishing and broadcasting on matters relating to food and drink. This is the twenty-eighth year of the Awards. An independent panel of judges selects thirteen category winners from work published or broadcast during the previous year.

The winner in each category receives £800, a case of Glenfiddich single malt Scotch whisky, and an engraved commemorative quaich.

The judges choose one outstanding candidate from the category winners to receive The Glenfiddich Trophy, to be held for one year, along with a further prize of £3,000.

Frequency	Annually
Closing date	31st January
Payment	£3,000 and Trophy

Gwyn Alf Williams Memorial Prize

Administrator	Welsh Academy
Address	3rd Floor, Mount Stuart House, Mount Stuart Square, Cardiff, CF1 6DQ
Phone number	01222 492025
Fax number	01222 492930
E.mail	dafr@celtic.co.uk
Entry fee	£5

Description

The award consists of a bursary of £3000 to include travel and expenses awarded each year. It is open to any writer or Welsh historian born or resident in Wales.

Frequency	Annually
Closing date	1st November
Payment	£3000

H E Bates Short Story Competition, The

Administrator	Northampton Borough Council
Address	Events Team, Cliftonville House, Bedford Road, Northampton
Phone number	01604 233500 ext 4243
Fax number	
E.mail	
Entry fee	£4

Description
Open to everyone.

1. Entries should be typed for preference and on one side of the paper only. A handwritten entry will not be excluded.

2. The story must not be of more than 2,000 words on any subject.

3. The organisers of this competition accept no responsibility for the loss or damage of any manuscript - please ensure you make a copy before submitting your entry.

Categories & Prizes

1. General:

Aged 16 years and over, 1st prize £200. Additional Prizes, including £50 for the best story written by a person resident in Northamptonshire.

2. Under 16:

1st Prize - gift voucher to the value of £25 plus a donation of £25 to the entrant's 'School Fund'.

3 .Under 11:

1st Prize - gift voucher to the value of £25 plus a donation of £25 to the entrant's 'School Fund'.

Frequency	Annually
Closing date	1st September
Payment	1st Prize - £200

Hawthornden Castle

Administrator	Adam Czerniawski
Address	Hawthornden Castle, Lasswade EH18 1EG
Phone number	0131 440 2180
Fax number	
E.mail	

Entry fee

Description
The Retreat provides a peaceful setting for five creative writers at a time working on a current project. Applications are invited from novelists, poets, dramatists and other creative writers of any nationality, who have published at least one book or similarly substantial piece of work. No monetary assistance is given, nor any contribution to travelling expenses, but once at Hawthornden, the writer is the guest of the Retreat for four weeks. Sessions are arranged in the periods February-July and September-December.

Frequency	Annually
Closing date	September
Payment	

Ian St James Award, The

Administrator	Merric Davidson
Address	P O Box 60, Cranbrook, Kent TN17 2ZR
Phone number	01580 212626
Fax number	01580 212041
E.mail	
Entry fee	£6

Description

The Ian St James Awards were created and launched by best-selling author, Ian St James, in 1988. Now in their ninth year, these annual Awards are recognised as one of the most prestigious, most relevant, international short story prizes for new writers previously unpublished in novel form. By 1997, through entering the ISJA, 102 first-time writers have been published in the annual book collections (the most recent being 'Pleasure Vessels' from Angela Royal Publishing) and over 200 runners-up published, first in Acclaim, and now The New Writer magazine. Many past Award winners have now gone on to become published novelists including Kate Atkinson, Louise Doughty, Mike McCormack, Anna McGrail. Entry forms are available in November.

Frequency	Annually
Closing date	30th April
Payment	Various amounts. Top Prize £2,000

Ilkley Literature Poetry Competition

Administrator	Alice Porter
Address	Manor House, 2 Castle Hill, Ilkley, LS29 9DT
Phone number	01943 601210
Fax number	01943 817079
E.mail	ilf@dial.pipex.com
Entry fee	£2.50

Description

A national competition with total prize money of over £600. This year's judge is O A Fanthorp who will present the prizes at the Ilkley Literature Festival's poetry day on October 12th, when winners will also have the opportunity to read their poem to an audience.

Frequency	Annually
Closing date	1st September
Payment	Prize fund: £600

International IMPAC Dublin Literary Award, The

Administrator	Brendan Teeling
Address	Dublin City Libraries, Cumberland House, Fenian Street, Dublin 2, Ireland
Phone number	+353 1 6619000
Fax number	+353 1 6761628
E.mail	dublin.city.libsoiol.ie

Entry fee

Description

An Award of £Ir100,000 is given annually for a novel which makes a lasting contribution to world literature. Nominations are made by selected libraries throughout the world and the Award is open to novels written in English or published originally in another language and also published in English translation. £Ir100,000 is awarded solely to the author if the work was originally published in English; if the book is in English translation the award is divided as £Ir75,000 to the author and £Ir25,000 to the translator. The inaugural winner was David Malouf for 'Remembering Babylon' (1996) and the 1997 winner was Javier Marias for 'A Heart So White' (translator - Margaret Jull Costa).

Frequency	Annually
Closing date	
Payment	£Ir100,000

Irish Times Literature Prize, The

Administrator	Gerard Cavanagh
Address	The Irish Times Literature Prizes, 10-16 D'Olier Street, Dubin 2
Phone number	003531 679 2022
Fax number	003531 670 9383
E.mail	gcavanagh@irish-times.ie

Entry fee

Description
The three winners of Irish Literature Prizes - for fiction, poetry and non-fiction prose - each receive £5,000, with £7,000 going to the author of the winning work in the International Fiction prize category. The international prize is for a work of fiction written in English and published in Ireland, Britain or the US, between 1st August, 1995 and 31st July 1997. Work eligible for the Irish Literature Prizes must be by an Irish author, published in Ireland, Britain or the US between 1st August 1995 and 1st July 1997 and can be in either English or Irish. Rules, conditions and other details of the prizes are available from the Administrator.

Frequency	Biennially
Closing date	
Payment	£22,000 Prize Fund

J R Ackerley Prize, The

Administrator	English PEN
Address	7 Dilke Street, London SW3 4JE
Phone number	0171 352 6303
Fax number	0171 351 0220
E.mail	

Entry fee

Description
The J R Ackerley Prize for Autobiography is awarded annually. Joe Ackerley left his royalties to a fund invested to provide capital for this purpose. The judges are the Trustees of the Fund. Neville Braybrooke, Michael Holroyd, Francis King, Peter Parker and Colin Spencer, who are looking for a literary autobiography written by an author of British nationality and published during that year.

Frequency	Annually
Closing date	
Payment	£2,000

James Tait Black Memorial Prizes

Administrator	Professor R D S Jack
Address	Department of English Literature, University of Edinburgh, David Hume Tower, George Square, Edinburgh, EH8 9JX
Phone number	0131 650 3619
Fax number	0131 650 6898
E.mail	s.strathdee@ed.ac.uk

Entry fee

Description

The James Tait Black Memorial Prizes, founded in memory of a partner in the publishing house of A & C Black Ltd, are one of the oldest and most prestigious book awards in Britain. Two prizes, each of £3000, are awarded annually: one for the best work of fiction, one for the best biography or work of that nature, published during the calendar year October 1st to September 30th. Publishers are invited to submit a copy of any work of fiction or biography which they judge may be considered for the award. In accordance with the wishes of the founder, eligible works are those written in English, originating with a British publisher, and first published in Britain in the 12 month period prior to the submission date (30th September). The nationality of the writer is irrelevant. Both prizes may go to the same author, but neither to the same author a second time. The prizes were first awarded in 1919.

Frequency	Annually
Closing date	30th September
Payment	2 prizes, each of £3000

John Masefield Memorial Trust, The

Administrator	The Society Of Authors
Address	84 Drayton Gardens, London, SW10 9SB
Phone number	0171 373 6642
Fax number	0171 373 5768
E.mail	authorsoc@writers.org.uk

Entry fee

Description
The Trust provides occasional grants to professional poets or their dependants who are faced with sudden financial problems.

Write for application form.

Frequency

Closing date

Payment

John Whiting Award

Administrator	Arts Council of England
Address	14 Great Peter Street, London SW1P 3NQ
Phone number	0171 973 6479
Fax number	0171 973 6590
E.mail	info.drama.ace@artfb.org.uk

Entry fee

Description
This annual award of £6,000 is intended to help further the careers and enhance the reputation of British playwrights.

Frequency	Annually
Closing date	
Payment	£6,000

K Blundell Trust, The

Administrator	The Society Of Authors
Address	84 Drayton Gardens, London, SW10 9SB
Phone number	0171 373 6642
Fax number	0171 373 5768
E.mail	authorsoc@writers.org.uk

Entry fee

Description

Eligibility:

At Miss Blundell's request, applicants must satisfy the following conditions:

1. they must be British by birth, ordinarily resident in the United Kingdom and under the age of 40 on the closing date for applications;

2. they must submit a copy of their latest book;

3. their work must 'contribute to the greater understanding of existing social and economic organisation'. Fiction is not excluded.

How to apply:

Application is made by letter (2-3 pages), including the following:

1. information about yourself and your books, as well as details of the book on which you are working;

2. information about your financial position with a full explanation as to why an award is needed and how it would be used;

3. confirmation that you satisfy the eligibility criteria specified by Miss Blundell;

4. copies of any recent reviews (not more than 2-3 pages on A4 paper - and not original newspaper cuttings);

5. submission of your latest book (which will be returned if a self-addressed label and stamps are enclosed).

Frequency   Annually

Closing date   30th April

Payment

Katherine Briggs Folklore Award, The

Administrator	The Folklore Society
Address	University College London, Gower Street, London, WC1E 6BT
Phone number	0171 387 5894
Fax number	
E.mail	

Entry fee

Description
The Katherine Briggs Folklore Book Award is awarded annually in memory of Katherine Briggs, eminent scholar and past president of the Folklore Society. The award is given by the Society to a book which is judged to make significant contribution to folklore studies. Books published between 1st June to the 31st May in the following year on all aspects of folk studies (folklore, ethnology, anthropology, art and related topics but excluding translations and material re-written for children) having their first or simultaneous publication in Britain can be considered for the award.

Frequency	Annually
Closing date	31st May
Payment	

Kent Literature Festival: Short Story Writing Competition

Administrator	Ann Fearey
Address	The Metropole Arts Centre, The Leas, Folkestone, Kent CT20 2LS
Phone number	01303 255070
Fax number	
Entry fee	£3.50

Description

The Beginning: If you are over 16 the challenge is to write a short story about any subject in less than 3,000 words.

The Middle: Send your form along with a cheque for £3.50 per entry to the Metropole Arts Centre, The Leas, Folkestone, Kent, CT20 2LS. The Judges, this year Diane Pearson, Michael Legat and Pamela Oldfield will then decide on a winner.

The End: You win a First Prize of £275, or a Second Prize of £150, or the Third Prize of £100 presented to you at our annual Award Ceremony held during the Kent Literature Festival.

Frequency	Annually
Closing date	25th July
Payment	£275

Kraszna-Krausz Book Awards

Administrator	Andrea Livingstone
Address	122 Fawnbrake Avenue, London SE24 0BZ
Phone number	0171 738 6701
Fax number	0171 738 6701
E.mail	

Entry fee

Description

Sponsored by the Kraszna-Krausz Foundation, these Awards are made to encourage and recognise outstanding achievements in the writing and publishing of books on the art, history, practice and technology of photography and the moving image.

The Awards are made annually with prizes for books on still photography alternating with those for books on the moving image. Entries in each year cover books published in the previous two years.

There are two main prizes of £10,000 each, and the judges may award special commendations of up to £1,000 for other finalists. Books published in any language, from publishers world-wide, are eligible.

Frequency	Annually
Closing date	1st July
Payment	£10,000

Kurt Maschler Award

Administrator	Book Trust
Address	Book House, 45 East Hill, London SW18 2QZ
Phone number	0181 870 9055
Fax number	0181 874 4790
E.mail	

Entry fee

Description
Awarded to the author and illustrator who have written a book which combines excellence in both text and illustration. Entries must be published in the calendar year of the award.

Frequency	Annually
Closing date	30th September
Payment	£1,000 and 'Emil' bronze figure

L Ron Hubbard's Writers Of The Future Contest

Administrator	Andrea Grant-Webb
Address	P O Box 218, East Grinstead, West Sussex RH19 4GH
Phone number	
Fax number	
E.mail	
Entry fee	Free

Description

Established in 1984, by top science fiction writer, L Ron Hubbard, to encourage new and amateur writers of science fiction, fantasy and horror. Entrants have to submit a short story of up to 10,000 words, or a novelette less than 17,000 words. Prizes £640, £480, and £320 each quarter for 1st, 2nd and 3rd place winners and an annual Grand Prize of £2,500. All the twelve yearly winners are awarded a trip to the annual L Ron Hubbard Achievement Awards, which include a series of professional writers' workshops; and are published in the 'L Ron Hubbard presents Writers of The Future' anthology.

Frequency	Quarterly with an annual Grand Prize
Closing date	31st Dec 97, 31st Mar 98, 30th Jun 98, 30th Sep 98
Payment	Grand Prize £2,500

Lakeland Book Of The Year Awards

Administrator	Sue Stewart
Address	Cumbria Tourist Board, Ashleigh, Holly Road, Windermere, LA23 2AQ
Phone number	01539 444444
Fax number	01539 444041
Entry fee	None

Description

Books published in the year prior to awards ceremony, Must be on any aspect relating to Cumbria - The Lake District.

Five prizes:

Hunter Davies: People/Places

Border TV: Illustrated

Barclays Bank Plc: Guide book

Tullie House Museum: History/environment

Jennings Bros: Small book

£100 prize and certificate. Awards luncheon in aid of local charity.

Frequency	Annually
Closing date	31st March
Payment	£100

Lancashire County Library/ National Westminster Bank Children's Book Of The Year Award

Administrator	Peter McKay
Address	Lancashire County Library HQ, 143 Corporation Street, Preston PR1 2UQ
Phone number	01772 264040
Fax number	01772 264880
E.mail	
Entry fee	Free

Description
Original fiction first published in UK between 1st September and 31st August each year. Author resident in UK. Collections of short stories by one author not published elsewhere are eligible.

Frequency	Annually
Closing date	31st August
Payment	£500 and engraved decanter

Lichfield Prize, The

Administrator	Lichfield District Council
Address	Frog Lane, Lichfield, Staffordshire
Phone number	01543 414000
Fax number	01543 250673
E.mail	

Entry fee

None

Description

The Prize of £5,000 and the opportunity of publication is awarded to the best new novel set in Lichfield District, an area with a rich literary heritage founded by such notables as Samuel Johnson, Erasmus Darwin and Elias Ashmole.

Entrants are invited to submit a work of fiction based historically or in the present day, with a story line set in the geographical area of Lichfield District in Staffordshire. The Prize is open to both new and existing authors. Judges look for a novel with a wide audience appeal which has the potential to become a best seller.

Frequency	Biennially
Closing date	To be determined
Payment	£5,000

Lloyds Private Banking Playwright Of The Year Award, The

Administrator	Tony Ball Associates Plc
Address	174-178 North Gower Street, London, NW1 2NB
Phone number	0171 380 0953
Fax number	0171 387 9004
E.mail	tba@tonyball.co.uk

Entry fee

Description

The Lloyds Private Banking Playwright of the Year Award is now in its fourth highly successful year. With a prize of £25,000 for the winner it makes the award one of the biggest sums ever given for an arts accolade.

The aim of the award is to encourage new and diverse playwrighting and broaden support for the theatre, particularly in the regions. The award has been designed to reward excellence and is given specifically for the style and quality of writing rather than the actual production itself.

The Judging Panel comprises senior national theatre critics and celebrity judges such as Nanette Newman and Ned Sherrin and is chaired by Melvin Bragg.

The Lloyds Private Banking Playwright of the Year Award is a natural extension of the Bank's established association with the Arts, for which they were most recently shortlisted for an ABSA award.

Frequency	Annually
Closing date	Potential Award nominations are assessed throughout the year by the Panel of Judges
Payment	£25,000

London Writers Competition

Administrator	Charlie Catling
Address	Room 254, Wandsworth Town Hall, Wandsworth High Street, London SW18 2PU
Phone number	0181 871 7380
Fax number	0181 871 7630
E.mail	
Entry fee	Short Story - £4.00 Poem £2.00

Description

Annual competition for writers working in Greater London. It comprises of two sections - poetry and short stories. The poetry section is for work up to 50 lines, the story section between 2000 and 5000 words.

Chairman of Judges: Martyn Goff OBE

The competition has been running for 21 years.

Prizes - 1st £600, 2nd £250, 3rd £100

Frequency	Annually
Closing date	July
Payment	£600

Macmillan Prize For Children's Picture Book Illustration, The

Administrator	Marketing Department
Address	Macmillan Children's Books, 25 Eccleston Place, London, SW1W 9NF
Phone number	0171 881 8000
Fax number	0171 881 8001
E.mail	

Description

The Macmillan Prize, funded by Macmillan Children's Books, a division of Macmillan Publishers, was established in order to stimulate new work from young illustrators in art schools and to help them start their professional lives. The competition is open to all art students in higher education establishments in the United Kingdom.

The competition is for a series of outstanding illustrations which show that the artist understands how to match pictures to text. The pictures should also demonstrate the entrant's grasp of narrative, pacing and characterisation.

The prizes will be awarded for work which the jury considers to be an original contribution to the field, and which children will enjoy. The first prize will be £1,000. The second and third prizes will be £500 and £250 respectively.

For further details and an entry form, please contact the Marketing Department, Macmillan Children's Books.

Frequency	Annually
Closing date	Early April
Payment	£1,000

Macmillan Silver Pen Award for Fiction, The

Administrator	Englih PEN
Address	7 Dilke Street, London, SW3 4JE
Phone number	0171 352 6303
Fax number	0171 351 0220
E.mail	

Entry fee

Description
The Macmillan Silver Pen Award, £500 and a silver pen, is sponsored by Macmillan and given to what, in the opinion of the judges, is an outstanding collection of short stories, written in English by an author of British nationality and published in the United Kingdom.

Frequency	Annually
Closing date	
Payment	£500 and silver pen

Margaret Rhondda Award, The

Administrator	The Society of Authors
Address	84 Drayton Gardens, London SW10 9SB
Phone number	0171 373 6642
Fax number	0171 373 5768
E.mail	authorsoc@writers.org.uk

Entry fee

Description

Friends of Lady Rhondda established a Trust to assist and support women journalists who are in needy circumstances by the provision of grants and awards in recognition of the service which they give to the public through their work in the field of journalism.

It will be given to a woman writer as a grant-in-aid towards the expenses of a research project in journalism. The grant, which may be divided, will not exceed one thousand pounds.

Applicants, who must be British or Commonwealth citizens ordinarily resident in Great Britain, should send:

a. details of their proposed project and a statement of the expenses to be covered by the grant.

b. details of past work, with one or two examples.

c. details of age, place of birth and normal place of residence.

d. a stamped addressed envelope for the return to the mss.

Candidates may be required to attend for interview.

Frequency	Every 3 years
Closing date	December
Payment	£1,000 (maximum)

Marsh Award For Children's Literature In Translation

Administrator	Author's Club
Address	40 Dover Street, London W1X 3RB
Phone number	0171 499 8581
Fax number	0171 409 0913
E.mail	

Entry fee

Description
Contact: Mrs Ann Carter

Established 1995 and sponsored by the Marsh Christian Trust, the award aims to encourage translation of foreign children's books into English. It is a biennial award (first year: 1996), open to British translators of books for 4-16 year-olds, published in the UK by a British publisher. Any category will be considered with the exception of encyclopaedias and reference. No electronic books.

Frequency	Biennially
Closing date	
Payment	£750

Marsh Biography Award

Administrator	Authors' Club
Address	40 Dover Street, London W1X 3RB
Phone number	0171 499 8581
Fax number	0171 409 0913
E.mail	

Entry fee

Description
Contact Mrs Ann Carter

A biennial award for the most significant biography published over a two-year period by a British publisher.

Frequency	Biennially
Closing date	
Payment	£3500 + Silver Trophy

Mary And Alfred Wilkins International Memorial Poetry Competition

Administrator	Philip A St John Fisher
Address	Birmingham and Midland Institute, 9 Margaret Street, Birmingham, B8 3BS
Phone number	0121 236 3591
Fax number	0121 212 4577
E.mail	
Entry fee	£3.00 per poem

Description
Annual poetry competition.

Prizes 1st £1000, 2nd £500, 3rd £200, 4th £100 plus five prizes of £20 and 10 prizes of £10

Adjudicators: Professor Susan Bassnett, Warwick University; Tobias Hill; David Dabydeen

Poems submitted must be in English, unpublished, and should not have been accepted for publication elsewhere. They should not have been entered for any other Poetry Competition.

Entries should not exceed 40 lines in length. A competitor may submit more than one entry provided that each is accompanied by the fee of £3.

The Organisers reserve the right to withhold award of all or any of the prizes if in the opinion of the Adjudicators, the standard of entry is not sufficiently high to justify awards.

Application forms from Birmingham and Midland Institute

Frequency   Annually

Closing date   28th June

Payment   1st £1000

Mary Vaughan Jones Award, The

Administrator	Welsh Book Council.
Address	Castell Brychan, Aberystwyth, Ceredigian, SY23 2JB
Phone number	01970 624151
Fax number	01970 625385
E.mail	

Entry fee

Description
Mary Vaughan Jones was one of the main benefactors of children's literature in Wales for a period of over thirty years. She was an infant teacher for fifteen years in the first official Welsh-language school and then a lecturer in infant methods in a Teachers' Training College. In recent years she was crippled with arthritis and more or less confined to her home but she continued to write for younger children right up to her death in early 1983. She wrote nearly forty books for children, one of the most popular is '

i Mali', her first book in a learning to read series for younger children. Thousands of children whose native language or second language is Welsh, will have learnt to read with 'Sali Mali' and a sales figure of nearly 40,000 over the last twenty years is a record in a minority language.

She also created the reading series, 'Cyfres Dau Dau', a series of eight grades with a large and smaller book in each grade with the odd supplementary book of rhymes or simple plays based on the same characters. She also undertook translation work, her best perhaps being the Welsh version of Tamasin Cole's 'Fourteen Rats and a Rat Catcher' and Pat Hutchins' 'Rosie's Walk'.

The award is a tribute to Mary Vaughan Jones for her outstanding contribution to children's books in the Welsh language.

The award is available for presentations every three years to a person who has made an outstanding contribution to children's literature in the Welsh language over a considerable period of time. The award is in a form of a silver trophy depicting characters from Mary Vaughan Jones's Books.

Frequency   Every Three Years

Closing date

Payment   Silver Trophy

MCA Book Prize

Administrator	Andrea Livingstone
Address	122 Fawnbrake Avenue, London SE24 0BZ
Phone number	0171 738 6701
Fax number	0171 738 6701
E.mail	
Entry fee	None

Description

The Management Consultancies Association (MCA) sponsors an annual book prize for the best management book of the year by a British writer. The prize aims to encourage and reward writers whose books contribute stimulating, original and progressive ideas on management issues. There is a main prize of £5,000 for the best book on a management related subject published in the calendar year. In addition, a special commendation for younger writers, carrying an award of £2,000, may be made to the author under 40 who has written the best published management book of the year.

Frequency	Annually
Closing date	15th November
Payment	£5,000

McKitterick Prize, The

Administrator	The Society of Authors
Address	84 Drayton Gardens, London SW10 9SB

Phone number	0171 373 6642
Fax number	0171 373 5768
E.mail	authorsoc@writers.org.uk

Entry fee

Description

The McKitterick Prize, generously endowed by the late T E M McKitterick, is for the benefit of authors over the age of forty and will be given on the strength of a first novel (whether published or unpublished).

Eligibility:

a. On 31st December the author of a work submitted must:

i) have passed his/her fortieth birthday; and

ii) not have had any adult novel published in any language (other than the one submitted).

b. The work submitted must:

i) be a full-length work in the English language (and not a translation) by one author;

and

ii) be a work of 'fiction or imagination or substantially of fiction or imagination';

and

iii) have been first published in the UK that year or be unpublished.

iv) if unpublished, not to have been previously submitted for the McKitterick Prize.

Frequency	Annually
Closing date	December
Payment	£4,000

Meyer-Whitworth Award

Administrator	Arts Council of England
Address	14 Great Peter Street, London SW1P 3NQ
Phone number	0171 973 6480
Fax number	0171 973 6590
E.mail	Info.drama.ace@artsfb.org.uk

Entry fee

Description
An award of £8,000. It is intended to help further the careers of UK playwrights who are not yet established.

Frequency

Closing date

Payment   £8,000

Michael Breathnact Literary Memorial Fund, The

Administrator	Clo Iar-Chonnachta
Address	Indreabhan, Co na Gaillimhe, Eire
Phone number	+ 353 91 593307
Fax number	+ 353 91 593362
E.mail	cic@iol.ie
Entry fee	Ir £10

Description

A prize of £1,000 will be presented annually. The competition is open to writers under 30 years of age for the best work in any literary form (i.e. novel, drama, poetry collection or short story collection) in the Irish language.

Frequency	Annually
Closing date	1st December 1997
Payment	£1,000

MIND Book Of The Year

Administrator	Anny Bracky
Address	Granta House, 15-19 Braodway, London, E15 4BQ
Phone number	0181 519 2122
Fax number	0181 522 1725
E.mail	

Entry fee

Description
Mind Book of the Year/ Allen Lane Award is awarded to works of fiction or non-fiction which deal with the experience of emotional distress and create a deeper understanding of mental health problems

Frequency	Annually
Closing date	31st December
Payment	£1,000

MIND Journalist Of The Year

Administrator   Anny Bracky

Address   Granta House, 15-19 Broadway, London,
                    E15 4BQ

Phone number   0181 519 2122

Fax number   0181 522 1725

E.mail

Entry fee

Description
Mind Journalist of the Year is awarded to the journalist who has consistently reported fairly on mental health problems or has produced an insightful article on the subject

Frequency   Annually

Closing date   31st December

Payment

Mitchell Prize, The

Administrator	Caroline Elam
Address	c/o Burlington Magazine, 14-16 Duke's Road, London
Phone number	0171 388 8157
Fax number	0171 388 1230
E.mail	burlington@compuserve.com
Entry fee	None

Description
This is not a grant or bursary but a book prize. Entry is free, nominations are usually put forward by publishers but authors could nominate books. The Mitchell prize is $15,000 awarded to a book that has made an outstanding contribution to art history - the Eric Mitchell prize is $5,000 awarded to a first book that has made an outstanding contribution to art history.

Frequency	Annually
Closing date	For nominations usually April (but tends to be flexible)
Payment	$20,000 Prize fund.

National Poetry Foundation Grants

Administrator   National Poetry Foundation

Address   27 Mill Road, Fareham, Hants PO16 0TH

Phone number   01329 822218

Fax number   01329 822218

E.mail

Entry fee

Description
These are given in a very specific range of areas to outlets that are to benefit poetry and poets on a national level, anyone may apply for such a grant. We do not advertise them.

Frequency

Closing date

Payment

New London Writers' Awards

Administrator	London Arts Board
Address	Elme House, 133 Long Acre, Covent Garden, London, WC2E 9AF
Phone number	0171 240 1313
Fax number	0171 240 4580
E.mail	jhn@lonab.demon.co.uk

Entry fee

Description
Who can apply

1 Writers can be of any nationality but must be resident in Greater London

2 Writers must have published one book of fiction or full-length poetry collection and no more (pamphlets are not taken into consideration)

3 Writers must show evidence of a work in progress, need for financial assistance and a plan for how such a bursary would be used

4 The first work in progress must be English or English translation

5 Writers whose first work is poetry and whose work in progress is fiction, and vice-versa

Frequency	Annually
Closing date	16th January
Payment	£3,500

Newspaper Press Fund

Administrator	Peter Evans - Director & Secretary
Address	Dickens House, 35 Wathen Road, Dorking, Surrey RH4 1JY
Phone number	01306 887511
Fax number	01306 876104
Entry fee	Life Membership £50

Description

If you are British or Irish, under the age of 60, and have been earning your living on the editorial side of a newspaper, television or radio for at least two years - you are almost certainly eligible to join.

Foreign journalists working for British companies, and living in the UK, are also eligible to join.

The NPF is especially relevant to the freelance journalists, whose application should show where his/her work is used.

The NPF provides help in times of sickness, unemployment, misfortune and old age. Grants can be made to unemployed people who have unusual difficulties or commitments. The NPF can often assist when help from other sources is not available.

The Fund's panel of medical consultants offers expert advice to members and dependants. This service can provide that vital second opinion which many people require when health problems arise.

At Dorking the Fund has a unique housing scheme created exclusively for retired journalists and their dependants. In delightful surroundings there are sheltered flats and bungalows; also a comfortable care home nearby for holidays and permanent residency.

Nobel Prize, The

Administrator	The Nobel Foundation
Address	Box 5232, Sturegatan 14, Stockholm, Sweden, S-10245
Phone number	00 46 8 663 0920
Fax number	00 46 8 660 3847
E.mail	

Entry fee

Description
Awarded yearly for outstanding achievement in physics, chemistry, physiology or medicine, literature and peace. Founded by Alfred Nobel, a chemist who proved his creative ability by inventing dynamite. In general, individuals cannot nominate someone for a Nobel Prize. The rules vary from prize to prize but the following are eligible to do so for Literature: members of the Swedish Academy and of other academies, institutions and societies similar to it in membership and aims; professors of history of literature or of languages at universities or colleges; Nobel Laureates in Literature; presidents of authors' organisations which are representative of the literary activities of their respective countries.

Frequency	Annually
Closing date	
Payment	£700,000

Northern Arts Literary Fellowship

Administrator	Chrissie Glazebrook
Address	9-10 Osbourne Terrace, Jesmond, Newcastle upon Tyne, NE2 1NZ
Phone number	0191 281 6334
Fax number	0191 281 3276
E.mail	cgk@norab.demon.co.uk

Entry fee

Description

The Northern Arts Literary Fellowship at the University of Durham and Newcastle upon Tyne was founded in 1967. Valued at £15,000 pa, the Fellowship is designed to create time for new work and to stimulate literary interests in each university and in the wider community. The post is tenable for 2 years. Applicants should be established writers with a strong record, and must be prepared to commit themselves to residence in the Northern region for the period of the Fellowship. The current Fellow is fiction writer Bridget O'Connor (1996-1998). Advertising for the next fellow is likely to take place in early 1998.

Frequency	Biennially
Closing date	Varies - will be advertised in The Guardian
Payment	£15,000 p.a.

Northern Arts Writers Awards

Administrator	Chrissie Glazebrook
Address	9-10 Osbourne Terrace, Jesmond, Newcastle upon Tyne, NE2 1NZ
Phone number	0191 281 6334
Fax number	0191 281 3276
E.mail	cgk@norab.demon.co.uk

Entry fee

Description
Annual awards open to writers living in the Northern Arts region (Co. Durham, Cumbria, Northumberland, Teeside and Tyne and Wear)

1 Cash award for published writers to 'buy time' to concentrate on a specific literary project.

2 Tyrone Guthrie Centre residency - a month in Northern Ireland for a published writer to devote time to writing free from everyday distractions.

3 Arvon Foundation creative writing courses - an opportunity for unpublished writers to attend a course of their choice at one of the Arvon Foundation centres.

Frequency	Annually
Closing date	August
Payment	

Open Poetry Competition

Administrator	Carmarthen Writers' Circle
Address	79 Bronwydd Road, Carmarthen, Dyfed SA31 2AP
Phone number	01267 230900
Fax number	
E.mail	
Entry fee	£2

Description

Entrants may like to explore the focal idea of 'Then and Now'. This is not a title and poems may be on any subject. Poems longer than one column of A4 paper will be disqualified.

Frequency	Annually
Closing date	June
Payment	£100

Open Short Story Competition

Administrator	Carmarthen Writers' Circle
Address	79 Bronwydd Road, Carmarthen, Dyfed SA31 2AP
Phone number	01267 230900
Fax number	
E.mail	
Entry fee	£4

Description

Submit stories in English with a reading time of under 15 minutes (2,200 to 2,500 words).

The judges will look for stories suitable for broadcasting, well constructed and told.

Frequency	Annually
Closing date	March
Payment	£120

Oppenheim-John Downes Memorial Trust

Administrator	Ref 13
Address	36 Whitefriars Street. London, EC4Y 8BH
Phone number	0171 353 3040
Fax number	0171 583 2869
E.mail	

Entry fee

Description
The awards may be made to deserving artists of any kind whether writers, painters, sculptors, musicians, dancers, actors, craftsmen, inventors or artists of any comparable nature or description being unable effectively to pursue their vocation by reason of their poverty. Awards may be made to persons who are natural born British subjects born within Great Britain, Northern Ireland, the Channel Islands or the Isle of Man of parents both of whom are or were British subjects born within the British Isles and neither of whose parents was or is of colonial or overseas origin subsequent to the year 1900. Applicants must be over 30 years of age on December 1st in the year in which the application is made. Awards tend to be in the range of £200 to £1500

Frequency	Annually
Closing date	31st October
Payment	£200 - £1500

Orange Prize For Fiction

Administrator	Book Trust
Address	Book House, 45 East Hill, London, SW18 2QZ
Phone number	0181 870 9055
Fax number	0181 874 4790
E.mail	
Entry fee	None

Description

The prize is awarded to the woman who, in the opinion of the judges, has written the best full length novel that is eligible for the prize. Any full length novel, written in English by a woman of any nationality is eligible. Books from all genres are encouraged, but all books must be unified and substantial works written by a single author. Neither a book of short stories nor a novella is eligible. All entries must be published in the UK between 1st April and the following 31st March, but may have been published previously outside the UK.

Frequency	Annually
Closing date	December
Payment	£30,000 and 'Bessie' statue

Outposts

Administrator	M Dargitter
Address	Hippopotamus Press, 22 Whitewell Road, Frome, Somerset, BA11 4EL
Phone number	01373 466653
Fax number	
E.mail	

Entry fee £3

Description
Annual poetry competition for poems up to 60 lines

Frequency	Annually
Closing date	31st January
Payment	£900 prize fund

Peterloo Poets Open Poetry Competition

Administrator	Lynn Chambers
Address	2 Kelly Gardens, Calstock, Cornwall, PL18 9SA
Phone number	01822 833473
Fax number	
E.mail	
Entry fee	£4 per poem

Description

Now in its 12th year, the Peterloo Poets Open Poetry Competition is one of the leading three annual competitions in the UK. Entries are world-wide. It is essential to send an sae to receive an entry form and rules. Harry Chambers, publisher of the Peterloo Poets imprint, reads all the poems and supplies the 3 other judges - who change each year - with a shortlist of 100 poems from which they select the prizewinners.

Frequency	Annually
Closing date	2nd March
Payment	£2.000 Prize fund

Portico Prize, The

Administrator	Emma Marigliano
Address	The Portico Library & Gallery, 57 Mosley Street, Manchester, M2 3HY
Phone number	0161 236 6785
Fax number	0161 236 6803
E.mail	

Entry fee

Description

The £2,500 Portico Prize for literature is awarded biennially for a work of fiction or non-fiction published between August of the previous prize and August of the current year. The work must be of general interest, literary merit and set wholly or mainly in the NW of England (the cities of Manchester and Liverpool, the surrounding countries of Lancashire and Cheshire, the High Peak area and the county of Cumbria).

Five judges (a bookseller, a librarian, a publisher, a writer and a local personality) select the winner, and the £2,500 prize is presented at a black-tie dinner in Manchester in November.

Frequency	Biennially
Closing date	August to August within the two years.
Payment	£2,500

Questors National Student Playwrighting Competition, The

Administrator	The Questors Theatre Playhouse.
Address	12 Mattock Lane, London W5 5BD
Phone number	0181 567 0011
Fax number	0181 567 8736
E.mail	

Entry fee

Description

£1,000 for the best play written by a full-time University or College student. The winning play is performed at The Questors Theatre Playhouse for one week. The judges include Dame Judi Dench (President of The Questors Theatre), Michael Williams and Oliver Ford Davies (Vice-Presidents). The Competition is open to full-time students in the UK. The Questors Theatre produces some 24 productions each year in its Playhouse and Studio Theatres.

Frequency	Annually
Closing date	
Payment	£1,000

Ralph Lewis Award

Administrator	Librarian & Director Of Information Services
Address	University of Sussex, Brighton, East Sussex, BN1 9QL
Phone number	01273 678 158
Fax number	01273 678 441
E.mail	a.n.peasgood@uk.ac.sussex.central

Entry fee None

Description

A monetary prize is awarded to support an approved 3 year programme of publishing new writing.

Established in 1984 by a bequest of Ralph Henry Lewis, author and art dealer of Brighton.

Frequency	Approx. 3 years
Closing date	
Payment	

Raymond Williams Community Publishing Prizes, The

Administrator	Literature Dept
Address	Arts Council of England, 14 Great Peter Street, London, SW1P 3NQ
Phone number	0171 333 0100
Fax number	
E.mail	

Entry fee

Description

Founded in 1990, these annual prizes are awarded to non-profitmaking publishers for work which offers outstanding imaginative and creative qualities and which exemplifies the values of ordinary people and their lives. First prize £2000 to publisher, £1000 to writer/group; Runner-up £1500 to publisher, £500 to writer/group.

Frequency	Annually
Closing date	30th April
Payment	1st £1000

Reginald Taylor & Lord Fletcher Essay Prize

Administrator	Dr Martin Henig
Address	c/o Institute of Archaeology, 36 Beaumont Street, Oxford

Phone number

Fax number

E.mail

Entry fee

Description

Reginald Taylor & Lord Fletcher Essay Prize is awarded biennially for the best unpublished essay submitted during the two-year period. The essay, not exceeding 7,500 words in length, must be of high academic and literary quality and demonstrate original research on a subject of archaeological, art-historical or antiquarian interest within the period from the Roman era to AD 1830. The prize is now included in the British Archaeological Awards scheme and the presentation will be made along with the other awards in November.

The successful competitor will be invited to read the essay before the Association and it may be published in the Journal of the Association, if approved by the Editorial Committee.

Frequency	Biennially
Closing date	1st June
Payment	£300 + Medal

Rhyme International

Administrator	Mike Shields
Address	27 Valley View, Primrose, Jarrow, Tyne and Wear, NE32 4QT
Phone number	0191 4897055
Fax number	
E.mail	
Entry fee	£2.50 per poem

Description

The only international competition exclusively for rhymed poetry. Has been running for 16 years and paid out over £16,000 in prizes

Frequency	Annually
Closing date	30th September
Payment	Average annual prize fund £1000

Rooney Prize For Irish Literarure

Administrator	Jim Sherwin - Chairman
Address	Strathin, Temple-Carrig, Delgany, Co. Wicklow, Ireland
Phone number	353 1 287 4769
Fax number	353 1 287 2595
E.mail	
Entry fee	None

Description

The Rooney Prize for Irish Literature is awarded to a different person each year. It is a non-competitive prize and its main aim is to reward and encourage young Irish writing talent. There is no application procedure and no entry form. To be considered, a writer must be Irish, published in either Irish or English and be under 40 years of age.

Frequency	Annually
Closing date	
Payment	£5,000

Rosemary Arthur Award, The

Administrator	National Poetry Foundation
Address	27 Mill Road, Fareham, Hants PO16 0TH
Phone number	01329 822218
Fax number	01329 822218
E.mail	

Entry fee £5

Description

This is an annual award open to anyone, with the winner announced on February 3rd each year. The prize consists of:

a. Publication by the NPF of a perfectly bound book of the winner's poems.

b. A suitably engraved brass and glass carriage clock.

c. £100 in cash.

To be eligible for the award the entrant must not have previously had a book of poetry published nor have self-published such a book.

Before December 31st each year an entrant must send 40 pages of poetry with a suitably stamped sae (or enough IPCs from those abroad) for the return of the work and results, together with a £5 reading fee (Sterling Money Order only from abroad) to the above address.

Frequency	Annually
Closing date	December
Payment	£100 and carriage clock

Royal Historical Society Award, The

Administrator	Joy McCartny
Address	University of London, Gower Street, London, WC1E 6BT
Phone number	0171 387 7532
Fax number	0171 387 7532

Entry fee

Description
The award will be awarded to the wrier of the best essay on a subject, to be selected by the candidate, dealing with Scottish history, provided such subject has been previously submitted to and approved by the Council of The Royal Historical Society. All person desirous of competing for the prize are invited to send in their essays to the Secretary of The Royal Historical Society.

The essay submitted must be a genuine work of research based on original (manuscript or printed) materials. The essay should be between 6000 and 10000 words in length (excluding foot-notes and appendices). It must be submitted in typescript. The author's name should not appear on the typescript and should be submitted separately. No person to whom the prize has been awarded may enter for any subsequent competition for the prize.

Frequency	Annually
Closing date	October
Payment	£250

Royal Literary Fund, The

Administrator	Mrs Fiona Clark
Address	144 Temple Chambers, Temple Avenue, London, EC4Y 0DA
Phone number	0171 353 7150
Fax number	0171 353 7150
E.mail	

Entry fee

Description

The Royal Literary Fund was founded in 1790 with the object of assisting published writers of approved literary merit. In certain circumstances, the dependant of a writer may receive a one-off grant.

Applicants have to submit examples of their work, in English, to be read by two members of the Committee for assessment of literary merit. If this is approved, the question of need is considered, with information gathered from the application form and from a visit by the Secretary. Grants and Pensions amounting to £677,509 were given to individual authors in the year 1996-1997.

Frequency

Closing date

Payment

Runciman Award, The

Administrator	Anglo-Hellenic League.
Address	Flat 4, 68 Elm Park Gardens, London SW10 9PB
Phone number	0171 352 2676
Fax number	
E.mail	None

Entry fee

Description

The Anglo-Hellenic League annually offers prizes, known as The Runciman Award in honour of Sir Steven Runciman, for works wholly or mainly about some aspect of Greece or the Hellenic scene, which have been published in their first English edition in the United Kingdom during that year and listed in Whitaker's Books In Print.

Thanks to the great generosity of the Onassis Foundation, which funds the Award, prizes are offered for works in three historical categories.

a) Greece from earliest times to the foundation of Constantinople, capital of the Roman Empire at   Byzantium, in 324

b) Byzantium and post-Byzantium from 324 until 1821

c) The modern Hellenic world from 1821 to the present

Awards may be given for a work of fiction, drama or non-fiction; concerned academically or non-academically with the history of any period; biography or auto-biography, the arts, archaeology; a guide book or a translation from the Greek of any period.

A prize of up to £3000 is offered in each category. The panel of judges may decide not to award prizes in one category or may wish to award extra prize money in one or more of the other categories. A book may cover two, or even all three, categories. How such a prize-winning book is categorised or how the money, up to a total of £9000, is awarded is entirely the responsibility of the judges.

Frequency   Annually

Closing date   Usually early February - can vary

Payment   Prizes up to £9,000

S T Dupont Gold Pen Award, The

Administrator	English PEN
Address	7 Dilke Street, London SW3 4JE
Phone number	0171 352 6303
Fax number	0171 351 0220
E.mail	

Entry fee

Description

The S T Dupont Gold Pen Award for Distinguished Service to Literature:

S T Dupont of Paris have designed a special gold pen for presentation to an author whose work has given both readers and writers pleasure and inspiration throughout his or her career.

Frequency	Annually
Closing date	
Payment	Gold pen

Saga Prize, The

Administrator	Book Trust
Address	Book House, 45 East Hill, London SW18 2QZ
Phone number	0181 870 9055
Fax number	0181 874 4790
E.mail	

Entry fee   £15

Description
Awarded to an unpublished manuscript by an author of black African descent. Authors must have been born, and reside, in the UK or the Republic of Ireland.

Frequency	Annually
Closing date	End of July
Payment	£3,000 and publication of manuscript

Sagittarius Prize, The

Administrator	The Society of Authors
Address	84 Drayton Gardens, London SW10 9SB

Phone number	0171 373 6642
Fax number	0171 373 5768
E.mail	authorsoc@writers.org.uk

Entry fee

Description

The Sagittarius Prize, sponsored by an anonymous benefactor, is for the benefit of authors over the age of 60 and will be given on the strength of a first published novel for adults.

Eligibility:

a. On 31 December the author of a work submitted must:

　i) have passed his/her sixtieth birthday; and

　ii) not have had any adult novel published in any language (other than the one submitted).

b. The work submitted must:

　i) be a full-length adult novel in the English language (and not a translation) by one author; and

　ii) have been first published in the UK (and not first published abroad) during that year.

Frequency	Annually
Closing date	December
Payment	£2,000

Salaman Prize For Non Fiction, The

Administrator	Ann Mitchell
Address	c/o Guppy's Enterprise Club, 17 Nunnery Lane, York
Phone number	01904 422464
Fax number	
E.mail	
Entry fee	£5

Description

The Salaman Prize is awarded to the author whose work, in the opinion of the judges, best exemplifies good non-fiction writing; that is, mastery of the subject and a clear and effective way of communication.

The book must have been published in the previous year. Open to any book or work of non-fiction on absolutely any subject. There must be a 'Northern' connection: either the subject of the work can be connected with the North of England, or the author should live or have been born in the North of England.

Frequency	Annually
Closing date	May
Payment	£150 cash; trophy; book tokens £50 by Blackwells Bookshop

Samuel Beckett Award, The

Administrator	Faber and Faber Limited Publishers
Address	3 Queen Square, London WC1N 3AU
Phone number	0171 465 0045
Fax number	0171 465 0034
E.mail	

Entry fee

Description

The aim of the award is to give support and encouragement to new playwrights at a crucial stage in their careers.

There will be two prizes of £1,500 each: one for the best first play for the stage, performed during the calendar year, and the other for the best first play for television performed in the same period. The award is sponsored by Channel 4, the Royal Court Theatre and Faber and Faber.

In addition the sponsors will, according to their resources and by mutual agreement, offer practical help to the winning writers in furthering their artistic careers.

Frequency	Annually
Closing date	
Payment	£1,500

Scottish Book Of The Year, The

Administrator	Mrs Kathleen Munro
Address	Saltire Society, 9 Fountain Close, 22 High Street, Edinburgh EH1 1TF
Phone number	0131 556 1836
Fax number	0131 557 1675
E.mail	

Entry fee

Description
Established 1982, the Award is open to authors of Scottish descent or living in Scotland, or for a book by anyone which deals with a Scottish topic. In 1988 the Award was extended to include the first published work by a new author. Entries are submitted by Literary Editors and publishers are invited to send relevant catalogues. Books published between 1st September and 31st August will be eligible.

Frequency	Annually
Closing date	
Payment	

Shiva Naipaul Memorial Prize, The

Administrator	Emma Bagnall
Address	The Spectator, 56 Doughty Street, London, WC1N 2LL
Phone number	0171 405 1706
Fax number	0171 242 0603
E.mail	

Entry fee

Description

This annual prize of £3,000 was founded in 1985 and is given to an English language writer of any nationality under the age of 35 for an essay of not more than 4,000 words describing a visit to a foreign place or people.

Frequency	Annually
Closing date	Early 1998
Payment	£3,000

Sir Bannister Fletcher Award

Administrator	Fletcher Award Committee
Address	RIBA, 66 Portland Place, London, W1N 4AD.
Phone number	0171 499 8581
Fax number	0171 409 0913
E.mail	

Entry fee

Description

This award was created by Sir Bannister Fletcher, who was president of Authors' Club for many years. The prize is donated by Nelson Hurst & Marsh, insurance brokers, and is presented annually for the best book on architecture or the fine arts published in the preceding year.

Frequency	Annually
Closing date	
Payment	£1000

Smarties Book Prize

Administrator	Book Trust
Address	Book House, 45 East Hill, London SW18 2QZ
Phone number	0181 870 9055
Fax number	0181 814 4790
E.mail	

Entry fee

Description

Awarded to a work of poetry or fiction written for children in age categories (0-5, 6-8, 9-11), The entry must be written in English by a UK citizen or an author resident in the UK. An adult panel will choose the shortlist, and the final winners in each category (Gold, Silver and Bronze) will be chosen by schoolchildren.

Frequency	Annually
Closing date	31st July
Payment	Gold = £2,500/Silver = £1,500/Bronze = £500

Somerset Maugham Awards, The

Administrator	The Society of Authors
Address	84 Drayton Gardens, London SW10 9SB
Phone number	0171 373 6642
Fax number	0171 373 5768
E.mail	authorsoc@writers.org.uk

Entry fee

Description

The Somerset Maugham Awards are given on the strength of the promise of a published work. The amount of the Awards is £5,000 each. The winners are required to use the money for a period or periods of foreign travel. It was Mr Maugham's intention that young writers should be able to enrich their writing by experience in foreign countries.

Poetry, Fiction, Criticism, Biography, History, Philosophy, Belles-Lettres and travel books are all eligible for the Awards. Dramatic works are not eligible.

Authors entering for the Awards must be British subjects by birth but not nationals of 'Eire or of any of the British Dominions'; ordinarily resident in the United Kingdom of Great Britain and Northern Ireland, and under the age of 35 at 31st December that year.

Frequency	Annually
Closing date	December
Payment	£5,000

Southport Writers' Circle

Administrator	Mrs Hilary Tinsley
Address	32 Dover Road, Birkdale, Southport, Merseyside, PR8 4TB
Phone number	
Fax number	
E.mail	
Entry fee	£1.50 first poem, £1.00 each additional poem.

Description

An international poetry competition with two categories - open and humour.

Frequency	Annually
Closing date	Postmarked 30th April
Payment	Prizes of £100, £50 and £25 in each category

Stakis Prize For The Scottish Writer Of The Year, The

Administrator	Book Trust Scotland
Address	Scottish Book Centre, 137 Dundee Street, Edinburgh EH11 1BG
Phone number	0131 229 3663
Fax number	0131 228 4293
E.mail	book.trust.scotland@dial.pipex.com

Entry fee

Description

Previously sponsored by McVities, The Stakis Prize for The Scottish Writer of the Year is Scotland's richest literary prize.

£10,000 for the winner, £1,000 each to the other four shortlisted writers.

Entries for the Prize must be published between 1st August and 31st July.

Frequency	Annually
Closing date	31st July
Payment	£10,000

Stand Magazine Poetry Competition

Administrator	Stand Magazine
Address	179 Wingrove Road, Newcastle upon Tyne NE4 9DA
Phone number	0191 273 3280
E.mail	
Entry fee	£3.50

Description

This first of Stand's Poetry Competitions is open to anyone in the world who can write poetry in English. It is open to the traditional poem as well as to every kind of experiment. The poem may presently be the orphan of literary forms, but some past winners of Stand's Competitions have gone to the ball and come back with a publisher, if not a prince. Some of the winning authors have subsequently published solo collections, some have been anthologised. It is in the hope of encouraging just such explorations and achievements that Stand now initiates its Poetry Competition. Good things lie ahead . . .

There will be a first prize of £1,500; a second of £500; a third of £250; a fourth of £150; a fifth of £100. There will also be 20 runners-up prizes of a one year subscription to Stand Magazine and Books from the prestigious Harper Collins Flamingo List, generously donated by the publisher. Reader's Digest will also donate a suitable volume.

Frequency	Biennially
Closing date	June
Payment	1st Prize £1,500

Stand Magazine Short Story Competition

Administrator	Stand Magazine
Address	179 Wingrove Road, Newcastle upon Tyne NE4 9DA
Phone number	0191 273 3280
Fax number	
Entry fee	£4.00

Description

This eighth Stand Short Story Competition is open to anyone in the world who can write fiction in English. It is open to the traditional short story as well as to every kind of experiment. The story may presently be the outcast of literary forms, but some past winners of Stand's Competitions have gone to the ball and come back with a publisher, if not with a prince! Some of the winning authors have subsequently published solo collections, some have been anthologised. It is in the hope of encouraging such explorations and achievements that Stand now offers its short fiction competition. Good things lie ahead . . .

There will be a first prize of £1,500; a second of £500; a third of £250; a fourth of £150; a fifth of £100. There will also be twenty runners-up of a one year subscription to Stand Magazine together with books generously donated by Harper Collins and Faber and Faber.

Frequency	Biennially
Closing date	June
Payment	1st Prize £1,500

Staple First Editions Award

Administrator	Donald Measham
Address	Tor Cottage, 81 Cavendish Road, Matlock, Derbyshire, DE4 3HD
Phone number	
Fax number	
E.mail	
Entry fee	£15 plus sae for return of typescript

Description
Poetry Collection and Prose Collection

Two single-author collections will be published during 1998-1999 as numbers 9 and 10 in the Staple First Editions series

The Editorial Board has the clear intention of selecting for publication one poetry and one fiction typescript (but reserves the right in exceptional circumstances to choose both from the same category).

Guaranteed circulation and sales to Staple subscribers; promotion and distribution to the book trade by Drake International Services and Bailey's of Kent.

Works must be original, written in English by a single author and consist entirely of either:

a) poetry, i.e. a collection or sequence of poems, or a single longer poem;

or

b) short fiction, i.e. several stories, or a single longer one.

The scale of work should be consistent with publication as a perfect bound booklet of around 32-48 pages of actual text. (note: for poetry, reckon 43 lines, including blank lines, per page. Prose, up to 450 words per page.)

Preparation of the submission is the author's responsibility. Staple cannot read longer works or offer pre-submission advice.

Send sae for full conditions: Entry form essential

Frequency	Biennially
Closing date	Postmarked by 1 February 1998
Payment	Publication and total £500 cash payment to authors, plus complimentaries and the option of discount copies. Plus refund of entry fee.

Stern Silver Pen, The

Administrator	English PEN
Address	7 Dilke Street, Chelsea, London SW3 4JE
Phone number	0171 352 3603
Fax number	0171 351 0220
E.mail	

Entry fee

Description
An annual award, the winner being nominated by the PEN Executive Committee, for an outstanding work of non-fiction written in English and published in England in the year preceding the prize, Previous winners: Susan Richards, Epics of Everyday Life; William St Clare, The Godwins and the Shelleys; Alan Bullock, Hitler and Stalin; Brian Keenan, An Evil Cradling.

Frequency	Annually
Closing date	
Payment	£500

Sunday Telegraph Catherine Pakenham Award, The

Administrator	Lucy Goodwin
Address	The Sunday Telegraph, 1 Canada Square, Canary Wharf, London, E14 5DT
Phone number	0171 538 6259
Fax number	0171 513 2512
E.mail	goodwinl@telegraph.co.uk
Entry fee	None

Description
The Catherine Packham Award is open to women journalists aged 18-25 who are resident in the UK. Entrants are asked to submit a non-fiction article of between 750-2000 words. Each entrant must have had a piece of writing published, however humble the publication. The article submitted for the award can be original or have already been published. The winner of the award will receive £1000 plus the opportunity to write for one of the Telegraph publications. Three runners-up will each receive £200. The winners will be presented with their prizes at a reception in London hosted by The Sunday Telegraph.

Frequency	Annually
Closing date	1st March
Payment	£1,000

Sunday Times Young Writer Of The Year, The

Administrator	The Society of Authors
Address	84 Drayton Gardens, London SW10 9SB
Phone number	0171 373 6642
Fax number	0171 373 5768
E.mail	authorsoc@writers.org.uk

Entry fee

Description
This award of £5,000 will be given on the strength of the promise shown by a full-length published work (fiction, non-fiction, plays or poetry).

a. The author of a work submitted must be:

    i) a British citizen ordinarily resident in Britain; and

    ii) under the age of 35 on 31st December that year.

b. The work submitted must be by one author in the English language and have first been published in Britain in that year.

Frequency	Annually
Closing date	31st December
Payment	£5,000

Theatre Writing Bursaries

Administrator	Arts Council of England
Address	14 Great Peter Street, London SW1P 3NQ
Phone number	0171 973 6479
Fax number	0171 973 6590
E.mail	info.drama.ace@artsfb.org.uk

Entry fee

Description
To provide experienced playwrights with an opportunity to research and develop a play for the theatre independently of financial pressures and free from the need to write for a particular market.

Frequency

Closing date

Payment

Thomas Cook/Daily Telegraph Travel Book Award

Administrator	Thomas Cook Publishing
Address	P O Box 227, Thorpe Wood, Peterborough, Cambridgeshire, PE3 6PU
Phone number	01733 503566
Fax number	01733 503596
E.mail	

Entry fee

Description
Annual award for books published in the English language, during the previous year, with the aim of encouraging and rewarding the art of literary travel writing.

Frequency	Annually
Closing date	30th April
Payment	£7,500

Times Educational Supplement Award, The

Administrator	Mrs Kathleen Munro
Address	Saltire Society, 9 Fountain Close, 22 High Street, Edinburgh EH1 1TF
Phone number	0131 556 1836
Fax number	0131 557 1675
E.mail	

Entry fee

Description
The Times Educational Supplement Award for Educational Publications

Established 1992 to encourage the best examples of published non-fiction work to enhance the teaching and learning of an aspect or aspects of the curriculum of Scottish schools. The work must be relevant to Scottish school children aged from 3-18.

Frequency	Annually
Closing date	31st October
Payment	

Tir Na N-Og Awards, The

Administrator	Welsh Books Council.
Address	Castell Brychan, Aberystwth, Ceredigion, SY23 2JB
Phone number	01970 624151
Fax number	01970 625385
E.mail	

Entry fee

Description

The main purpose of the Tir na n-Og awards is to raise the standard of children's and young people's books published during the year and to encourage the buying and reading of good books.

If in the opinion of the selection panel, there are books of sufficient merit, prizes will be awarded annually to acknowledge the work of authors and illustrators in the following three categories:

i) Welsh Fiction

Original Welsh language novels, stories and picture-books are considered. In books heavily dependent on illustrations the same detailed consideration is given to the visual element, and that could lead to sharing the prize between the author and the illustrator.

ii) Welsh Non-fiction

Every other Welsh language book published the relevant year is considered with the exception of those translations produced overseas in the form of international editions, and also packs and pamphlets.

iii) English Section

The best English language book of the year with an authentic Welsh background. Fiction and factual books originated in English are eligible. Translations from Welsh or any other language are not eligible.

Frequency   Annually

Closing date   31st December

Payment   £1000 in each category

Tom-Gallan Trust Award, The

Administrator	The Society Of Authors
Address	84 Drayton Gardens, London SW10 9SB
Phone number	0171 373 6642
Fax number	0171 373 5768
E.mail	anthorsoc@writers.org.uk

Entry fee

Description
An award, not to exceed one thousand pounds, is made biennially from the Fund to fiction writers of limited means who have had at least one short story accepted for publication.

Authors (who must be citizens of the United Kingdom, Commonwealth or the Republic of Ireland) wishing to enter should send:

1. A list of their already published fiction, giving the name of the publisher or periodical in each case and the approximate date of publication.

2. One short story in English (and not a translation) published or unpublished.

3. A brief statement of their financial position.

4. Date of birth.

5. An undertaking that they intend to devote a substantial amount of time to the writing of fiction as soon as they are financially able to do so.

6. A small stamped addressed envelope to acknowledge receipt, and another sae for the return of work submitted.

The judges will have in mind Miss Tom-Gallon's expressed preference for work of a traditional rather than of an experimental character.

Frequency	Biennially
Closing date	September
Payment	£1,000 (maximum)

Tony Godwin Memorial Trust, The

Administrator	Laurence Pollinger Limited
Address	18 Maddox Street, London W1R OEU
Phone number	0171 629 9761
Fax number	0171 629 9765
E.mail	i-brown@compuserve.com

Entry fee

Description

The Tony Godwin Award is open to all young people under the age of 35 who are UK nationals and working or intending to work in the book trade, and provides a bursary for the recipient to spend at least one month as the guest of a US publishing house. The bursary covers travel and living expenses only. It is not a holiday, but is designed to provide the opportunity for a promising individual to promote the British book trade and extend their skills and knowledge. Upon their return, the recipient is obliged to submit a written report identifying and exploring aspects of the American publishing scene for distribution throughout the international book trade.

The Award commemorates the outstanding contributions that Tony Godwin made to publishing in the 1960s and 1970s. He was a talented and energetic publisher, and was responsible for re-establishing Penguin Books as a major global publishing force. The work of Tony Godwin was characterised by the qualities of tremendous enthusiasm and ambition, intellectual excitement, political awareness, literary sensitivity and, above all, imagination. The Tony Godwin Award, founded by members of the international book trade following his sudden death in 1976, seeks to encourage similar qualities in young people in the UK book trade.

Frequency	Biennially
Closing date	31st December
Payment	A bursary of up to US$5,000

Travelling Scholarships, The

Administrator	The Society of Authors
Address	84 Drayton Gardens, London SW10 9SB
Phone number	0171 373 6642
Fax number	0171 373 5768
E.mail	authorsoc@writers.org.uk

Entry fee

Description
These awards were established in 1944 to enable British creative writers to keep in touch with their colleagues abroad, They are non-competitive and applications are not therefore required.

Frequency

Closing date

Payment

Trevor Reese Memorial Prize, The

Administrator	The Institute of Commonwealth Studies.
Address	University of London, 28 Russell Square, London, WC1B 5DS
Phone number	0171 580 5876
Fax number	0171 255 2160
E.mail	sjansen@sas.ac.uk

Entry fee

Description

Established in 1979 with the proceeds of contributions to a memorial fund to Dr Trevor Reese, Reader in Commonwealth Studies at the Institute of Commonwealth Studies, University of London, and a distinguished scholar of Imperial History (d. 1976). Biennial awards of £1000 for a scholarly work, usually by a single author, in the field of Imperial and Commonwealth History published in the preceding two years. The next award will be in 1998. Publishers or authors wishing to submit titles published in 1995 and 1996 for consideration for the 1998 award should send one copy to the Seminar and Conference Secretary, at the above address. No other form of entry is required.

Frequency	Biennially
Closing date	End of March
Payment	£1,000

UNESCO/PEN Short Story Competition, The

Administrator	English PEN
Address	7 Dilke Street, London SW3 4JE
Phone number	0171 352 6303
Fax number	0171 351 0220
E.mail	

Entry fee

Description
The prize, sponsored by UNESCO, is awarded to authors whose mother tongue is not English. Stories of a maximum length of 1,500 words are submitted through national PEN centres and three prizes are awarded of $3,000, $2,000 and $500.

Frequency	Annually
Closing date	
Payment	1st Prize $3,000

Unicorn National Young Playwright Competition

Administrator	Unicorn Arts Theatre
Address	6/7 Great Newport Street, London, WC2H 7JB
Phone number	0171 379 3280
Fax number	0171 836 5366
E.mail	

Entry fee

Description
1998 will mark the 11th Annual Young Playwright Competition. It is open to all children between the ages of 6-16 with 3 age groups: 6-8, 9-12 and 13-16. There is always a general theme around which the entrants should base their plays and let their imaginations run wild! This year the theme is 'secrets'. Entries may be submitted by individuals or groups of up to four, but the maximum number of pages is ten. Each year there are between 100 and 200 entries, which are read by a panel of celebrity judges. Adrian Mitchell, Tom Stoppard and Alan Ayckbourn have all been judges in the past. The winners, who are announced in February, will then receive several prizes, one of which will be a rehearsed reading of their play by a company of professional actors at the 'Unicorn Arts Theatre'. They will also be invited to writers' workshops with professional writers and directors offering advice, and where they can continue to work on their play or make changes as the actors rehearse it.

Applicants should write to Ruth Burgess at the Unicorn Arts Theatre for entry forms.

Frequency	Annually
Closing date	Early January

Ver Poets Open Competition

Administrator	May Badman
Address	Haycroft, 61-63 Chiswell Green Lane, St Albans, Hertfordshire, AL2 3AL
Phone number	01727 867005
Fax number	
E.mail	
Entry fee	£2.00 per poem.

Description

The Ver Poets Open Competition is an annual event which began in 1973. A total of £1000 in prizes is awarded as follows - First £500, Second £300, and two equal Third prizes of £100 each. The winner and about 30 selected poems are published in the anthology, 'Vision On'. Invited to adjudicate each year are well-known poets including George Szirtes, Roger Garfitt, Lawrence Sail, Carole Satyamurti.

Entrants are requested to use a pseudonym on their poems and to complete an entry form with their real name and address. The competition is open to members of Ver Poets and also non-members, and entries are accepted from countries abroad. We ask for unpublished work in English of no more than 30 lines. Prize winners have included well-known and previously unknown writers.

Frequency	Annually
Closing date	30th April
Payment	£1,000 Prize fund.

Verity Bangate Award

Administrator	Soho Theatre Company
Address	21 Dean Street, London, W1V 6NE
Phone number	0171 287 5060
Fax number	0171 287 5061
E.mail	sohotheatre.co.uk

Entry fee

Description

The award is open to any author resident in the British Isles for an original play written in English. Plays should be full length, professionally unperformed, suitable for studio theatre production and uncumbered by any third party rights. Plays should be clearly typed with wide margins. Each submitted play should have a title page which states the author's name and address alongside the name of the play and be accompanied by two sae's, one for an acknowledgement letter and one for the return of the script. Prize winners are expected to attend a ceremony later in the year. The judges' decision is final and no correspondence concerning the result can be entered into. Playwrights with three or more professional productions to their credit; plays commissioned by Soho Theatre Company; previous Verity Bangate Award winners are not eligible.

Frequency	Biennially
Closing date	To be announced
Payment	First Prize £1500.

W H Heinemann Prize, The

Administrator	The Royal Society of Literature
Address	1 Hyde Park Gardens, London, W2 2LT
Phone number	0171 723 5104
Fax number	0171 402 0199
E.mail	
Entry fee	None

Description
Founded in 1944, the purpose of the bequest is the encouragement of genuine contribution to literature. The testator wished the jury to give preference to those publications which are less likely to command big sales - e.g. poetry, biography, criticism, history; though novels, if of sufficient distinction, would not be overlooked. One, two or three prizes may be given, though the jury reserves the right to withhold an award if no work is submitted which, in their opinion, is of sufficient merit.

Frequency	Annually
Closing date	31st October.
Payment	

Welsh Academy Young Writers' Competition

Administrator	Welsh Academy
Address	3rd Floor, Mount Stuart House, Mount Stuart Square, Cardiff, CF1 6DQ.
Phone number	01222 492025
Fax number	01222 492930
E.mail	dafr@celtic.co.uk |//
Entry fee	None

Description
6 Categories:

Up to 11 yrs poetry and prose,

12-15 yrs poetry and prose,

16-18 yrs poetry and prose,

Extra prize for 16-18 to write a journalistic piece on devolution.

For further details please send to: PO Box 328, Cardiff, CF2 1XL.

Frequency	Annually
Closing date	14th November
Payment	£1,000

West Midlands Arts

Administrator   Information Services

Address   82 Granville Street, Birmingham, B1 2LH

Phone number   0121 631 3121

Fax number   0121 643 7239

E.mail   west.midarts@midnet.com

Entry fee

Description

Description. West Midlands Arts is the Regional Arts Board for Hereford and Worcester, Shropshire, Staffordshire, Warwickshire and the West Midlands Metropolitan Districts. Nationally, the ten Regional Arts Boards, with the Arts Council of England, the Crafts Council and the British Film Institute, are responsible for the funding and development of the arts council in England.

Policy. West Midlands Arts believes in making the difference. Committed to working with partners in the public, voluntary and private sectors, WMA supports the arts, crafts and media of the region through action in five areas: Funding, Advice, Information, Training and Planning, working with regional and national partners to increase resources and opportunities in the arts. New, innovative work is strongly encouraged, and WMA also aims to sustain and develop the region's network of key promoters. Despite limited resources, revenue and annual programme support are available to a small number of organisations, and various grant schemes are available annually to support performing arts and cross-artform projects. An advice service is available for those thinking of applying to the Arts Lottery, and the West Midlands holds the best record nationally in seeing Lottery bids through. Contact Information Services at WMA for details of information and advice services.

Whitfield Prize

Administrator	Royal Historical Society
Address	University College of London, Gower Street, London WC1E 6BT
Phone number	0171 387 7532
Fax number	0171 387 7532

Entry fee

Description

The Royal Historical Society annually offers the Whitfield Prize (value £1,000) for a new book on British history.

To be eligible for consideration for the prize the book must:

i. be on a subject within a field of British history;

ii. have been published in the United Kingdom during the year;

iii. be its author's first solely written history book;

iv. be an original and scholarly work of historical research.

The author or the publisher should submit three copies (non-returnable) of an eligible book by the end of the year.

Frequency	Annually
Closing date	End of December
Payment	£1,000

Winifred Holtby Prize, The

Administrator	The Royal Society of Literature
Address	1 Hyde Park Gardens, London, W2 2LT
Phone number	0171 723 5104
Fax number	0171 402 0199
E.mail	
Entry fee	None

Description

Founded in 1966 by Vera Brittain to honour the memory of Winifred Holtby, the prize is for the best regional novel of the year written in the English language. The writer must be of British or Irish nationality or a citizen of the Commonwealth. Translations, unless made by the author himself of his own work, are not eligible for consideration. If in any year it is considered that no regional novel is of sufficient merit, the prize may be awarded to an author, qualified as aforesaid, of a literary work of non-fiction or poetry, concerning a regional subject.

Frequency	Annually
Closing date	31st October
Payment	

Writers Bureau Poetry And Short Story Competition, The

Administrator	Angela Cox Competition Secretary
Address	The Writers Bureau, Sevendale House, 7 Dale Street, Manchester, M1 1JB
Phone number	0161 228 2362
Fax number	0161 228 3533
E.mail	
Entry fee	£3.50

Description

There is a first prize of £300, a second prize of £200, a third prize of £100, a fourth prize of £50 and a fifth prize of £25 in each category.

There is no limit to the number of entries provided each one is accompanied by a £3.50 entry fee. Cheques and postal orders should be made payable to The Writers Bureau.

Poems must not exceed 40 lines. Short stories must not exceed 2000 words. Entries must be typed. Work may be on any subject but should not have been previously published.

Entry forms available by sending sae.

Frequency	Annually
Closing date	31st July
Payment	£675 prize fund

Writers' Awards Scheme

Administrator	Arts Council of England
Address	14 Great Peter Street, London SW1P 3NQ
Phone number	0171 973 6442
Fax number	0171 973 6590
E.mail	info:literature.ace@artsfb.org.uk

Entry fee

Description
To provide 15 awards of £7,000 each to creative writers who have had at least one book previously published. Awarded annually, advertised in July.

Frequency	Annually
Closing date	
Payment	£7,000

Yorkshire Post Art And Music Book Award

Administrator	Yorkshire Post
Address	P O Box 168, Wellington Street, Leeds LS1 1RF
Phone number	0113 243 2701
Fax number	0113 238 8909
E.mail	

Entry fee

Description
Prizes of £1,000 are given to authors whose books, published in that year, are judged to have contributed most to the understanding and appreciation of Art/Music. It is immaterial where the book was printed provided the publishers are based in the UK.

Submissions are accepted only from publishers and up to four books in total (per imprint) may be submitted by any one publisher. The author should be British or resident in the UK. Translations, re-issues and works of a strictly scientific nature are excluded.

Frequency	Annually
Closing date	December
Payment	£1,000

Yorkshire Post Best First Work Award

Administrator	Yorkshire Post
Address	P O Box 168, Wellington Street, Leeds LS1 1RF
Phone number	0113 243 2701
Fax number	0113 238 8909
E.mail	

Entry fee

Description
Prize of £1,000 for the Best First Work by a new author (either fiction or non-fiction). Submissions are accepted only from publishers and up to four books in total (per imprint) may be submitted by any one publisher. The author should be British or resident in the UK. Translations, re-issues and works of a strictly scientific nature are excluded.

Frequency	Annually
Closing date	December
Payment	£1,000

Yorkshire Post Book Of The Year

Administrator	Yorkshire Post
Address	P O Box 168, Wellington Street, Leeds LS1 1RF
Phone number	0113 243 2701
Fax number	0113 238 8909

Entry fee

Description
Prize of £1,200 for the Best Book (either fiction or non-fiction) published in the UK during the year. Submissions are accepted only from publishers and up to four books in total (per imprint) may be submitted by any one publisher. The author should be British or resident in the UK. Translations, re-issues and works or a strictly scientific nature are excluded.

Frequency	Annually
Closing date	December
Payment	£1,200

award.

Frequency	Annually
Closing date	April/May
Payment	£315 Prize fund.

Airey Neave Research Award

The Airey Neave Trust, House of Commons,
London SW1A 0AA

- o -

An Duais Don Filiocht In Gaeilge

70 Merrion Square, Dublin 2, Eire

- o -

Andre Simon Memorial Fund Book Awards

61 Church Street, Isleworth, Middlesex, TW7 6BE

- o -

Angel Literary Prize

The Angel Hotel, Angel Hill, Bury St Edmonds,
Suffolk

- o -

Anne Frankel Prize

c/o Critics' Circle, 47 Bermondsey Street,
London, SE1 3XT

- o -

Anne Tibble Poetry Competition

Cliftonville House, Bedford Road, Northampton
- o -

Aosdana Scheme

70 Merrion Square, Dublin 2, Eire
- o -

Aristeion Prize, The

Commission of the EC, Culture Unit, Rue de la
Loi 200, B-1049, Brussels, Belgium
- o -

Arthur C Clarke Award

North East London Poly, Longbridge Road,
Dagenham, Essex, RM8 2AS
- o -

Arthur Markham Memorial Award

University of Sheffield, Western Bank,
Sheffield, South Yorkshire, S10 2TN
- o -

Arts Council Awards And Bursaries

Arts Council of England, 14 Great Peters Street, London SW1P 3NQ

- o -

Arts Council Theatre Writing Bursaries

14 Great Peter Street, London, SW1P 3NQ

- o -

Arvon Poetry Competition

Kilnhurst, Kilnhurst Road, Todmorden, Lancashire, OL14 6AX

- o -

Author Of The Year Award

272 Vauxhall Bridge Road, London, SW1V 1BA

- o -

Authors Foundation, The

84 Drayton Gardens, London, SW10 9SB

- o -

BAAL Book Prize

School of Education, The Open University,
Milton Keynes, Northamptonshire, MK7 6AA

- o -

BBC Wildlife Awards For Nature Writing

Broadcasting House, Whiteladies Road,
Bristol, BS8 2LR

- o -

Bernard Shaw Translators Prize

84 Drayton Gardens, London, SW10 9SB

- o -

Besterman Medal, The

7 Ridgemont Street, London WC1W 7AE

- o -

BFI Michael Powell Book Award

21 Stephen Street, London, W1P 1PL

- o -

Boardman Tasker Memorial Award

14 Pine Lodge, Dairyground Road, Bramhill,
Stockport, Cheshire, SK7 2HS
- o -

Bournemouth Open Poetry Competition

2 Digby Chambers Post Office Road,
Bournemouth, Dorset, BH1 1BA,
- o -

BP Conservation Book Prize, The

Book Trust, Book House, 45 East Hill, London,
SW18 2QZ
- o -

BP Conservation Book Trust

Book Trust, Book House, 45 East Hill, London
SW18 2QZ
- o -

Bridport Creative Writing Competition

South Street, Bridport, Dorset
- o -

British Academy Publications Subvention

20-21 Cornwall Terrace, London, NW1 4QP

- o -

British Academy Small Personal Research

20-21 Cornwall Terrace, London, NW1 4QP

- o -

British Book Awards

43 Museum Street, London, WC1A 1LY

- o -

British Book Design & Production Award

11 Bedford Row, London, WC1R 4DX

- o -

British C L A T Prize

St John's College, Oxford, OX1 3JP

- o -

British Press Award

Holborn Circus, London, EC1P 1DQ

- o -

British Science Fiction Awards

60 Bournemouth Road, Folkestone, Kent CT19 5AZ

- o -

Bursaries In Literature

70 Merrion Square, Dublin 2, Eire

- o -

Carey Award, The

16 Green Road, Birchington, Kent, CT7 9JZ

- o -

Carmarthen Writers' Circle Short Story Competition

79 Bronwydd Road, Carmerthen, Dyfed, SA31 2AP

- o -

Carnegie Medal, The

7 Ridgemont Street, London, WC1E 7AE
- o -

Cassell Award

Cassell plc, Wellington House, 125 Strand, London WC2R 0BB
- o -

Catherine Cookson Fiction Prize, The

61-63 Uxbridge Road, London, W5 5SA
- o -

Cheltenham Prize

c/o Town Hall, Imperial Square, Cheltenham, Gloucestershire, GL50 1QA
- o -

Children's Book Circle Eleanor Farjeon Award

c/o Macmillan Publishers Ltd, 25 Eccleston Place, London, SW1W 9ND
- o -

Children's Book Of The Year Award

143 Corporation Street, Preston, Lancashire,
PR1 2TB
- o -

Christopher Ewart-Biggs Memorial Prize

3/149 Hamilton Terrace, London, NW8 9QS
- o -

City Of Cardiff Poetry Competition

PO Box 438, Cardiff, CF1 6YA
- o -

Collins Biennial Religious Book Award

77-85 Fulham Place Road, London, W6 8JB
- o -

Collins Religious Book Award

77-85 Fulhan Palace Road, London W6 8JB
- o -

Commonwealth Writers' Prize

Marlborough House, Pall Mall, London, SW1Y 5HY

- o -

Constable Trophy, The

45 East Hill, London, SW18 2QZ

- o -

Crabbe Memorial Poetry Competition, The

Lowermead, Alphamstone, Nr Bures, West Suffolk, CO8 5HS

- o -

Creative Writing Junior Competition

Bridport Arts Centre, South Street, Bridport, Dorset DT6 3NR

- o -

Crime Writers' Association Awards

PO Box 172, Tring, Herts, HP23 5LP

- o -

D H Lawrence/GPT Short Story Competition

Technical & Leisure Services, Foster Avenue,
Beeston, Nottingham, NG9 1AB

- o -

Daily Telegraph National Power Young Science Writer Awards, The

334A Goswell Road, London EC1V 7LQ

- o -

David Berry Prize

University College London, Gower Street,
London, WC1E 6BT

- o -

David Cohen British Literature Prize

14 Great Peter Street, London, SW1P 3NQ

- o -

David Gemmell Cup

39 Emmanuel Road, Hastings, East Sussex,
TN34 3LB

- o -

Dennis Devlin Awards

70 Merrison Square, Dublin 2 Eire

- o -

Dennis Potter TV Play Of The Year, The

BBC Room D333, Centre House, 56 Wood Lane, London W12 7SB

- o -

Deo Gloria Award, The

45 East Hill, London, SW18 2QZ

- o -

Dillons First Fiction Award

Publicity Department, Royal House, Prince's Gate, Homer Road, Solihull, West Midlands, B91 3QQ

- o -

E Reginald Taylor Essay Competition

36 Beaumont Street, Oxford, Oxfordshire, OX1 2PG

- o -

Earthworm Award, The

26-28 Underwood Street, London, N17JQ

- o -

Eastern Arts Writing Fellowship

University of East Anglia, University Plain, Norwich, Norfolk, NR4 7JT

- o -

Economist/Richard Casement Internship, The

25 St James's Street, London, SW1A 1HG

- o -

Eileen Anderson Central TV Drama Award

Central Broadcasting, Central House, Broad Street, Birmingham, West Midlands, B1 2JP

- o -

Eric Mitchell Prize, The

c/o The Burlington Magazine, 14-16 Duke's Road, London, WC1H 9AD

- o -

Esquire/Waterstones Non-Fiction Award

Esquire, National Magazines Co, 72 Broadwick Street, London W1V 2BP

- o -

European Poetry Translation Prize

The Poetry Society, 22 Betterton Street, London WC2H 9BU

- o -

Fawcett Society Book Prize

46 Harleyford Road, London, SE11 5AY

- o -

FCI Essay Competition

Fan Circle International, Cronk-Y-Voddy, 21 Rectory Road, Coltishall NR12 7HF

- o -

Felicia Hemans Prize

University of Liverpool, PO Box 147, Liverpool, Merseyside, L69 3BX

- o -

Fulbright Chandler Fellowship

6 Porter Street, London, W1M 2HR
- o -

Fulbright TEB Clarke Fellowship

Fulbright House, 62 Doughty Street, London, WC1N 2LS
- o -

Garavi Gujarat Annual Book Award

Garavi Gujarat Publications Ltd, Garavi Gujarat House, 1-2 Silex Street, London SE1 0DW
- o -

Geoffrey Faber Memorial Prize

Faber & Faber Ltd, 3 Queen Square, London, WC1N 3AU
- o -

George Devine Award

17A South Villas, London, NW1 9BS
- o -

Gibb Memorial Trust

Delotte & Touche, Leda House, Station Road, Cambridge CB1 2RN

- o -

Glaxo Prizes For Medical Writing

Medical Writers Group, 84 Drayton Gardens, London, SW10 9SB

- o -

Greenwich Festival Poetry Competition

6 College Approach, Greenwich, London SE10 9HY

- o -

Griffith John Williams Memorial Prize

Welsh Academy, 3rd Floor, Mount Stuart House, Mount Stuart Square, Cardiff CF1 6DQ

- o -

H H Wingate/Jewish Quarterly Prizes

PO Box 1148, London, NW5 2AZ

- o -

Hans Christian Anderson Medals

45 East Hill, London, SW18 2QZ

- o -

Heinemann Award For Literature

The Royal Society of Literature, 1 Hyde Park Gardens, London W2 2LT

- o -

Heywood Hill Literary Prize

10 Curzon Street, London, W1Y 7FJ

- o -

Hunter Davies Prize

Ashleigh, Holly Road, Windermere, LA23 2AQ

- o -

Independent Award For Foreign Literature, The

40 City Road, London, EC1Y 2DB

- o -

Issac & Tamara Deutscher Memorial Prize

157 Fortis Green Road, London, N10 3AX

- o -

James Cameron Award

City University, Dept of Journalism,
Northampton Square, London, EC1V OHB

- o -

Jewish Quarterly Literary Prizes

PO Box 2078, London, W1A 1JR

- o -

John Florio Prize, The

84 Drayton Gardens, London, SW10 9SB

- o -

John Tripp Award

The Welsh Academy, 3rd Floor, Mount Stuart
House, Mount Stuart Square, Cardiff CF1 6DQ

- o -

Kent & Sussex Poetry Society Open Competition

8 Edward Street, Southborough, Tunbridge Wells, Kent, TN4 0HP

- o -

King George's Fund Award

1 Chesham Street, London, SW1X 8NF

- o -

Laurence Stren Fellowship

Graduate Centre For Journalism, City University, Northampton Square, London, EC1V 0HB

- o -

Leek Arts Poetry Competition

44 Rudyard Road, Biddulph Moor, Stoke-on-Trent, Staffs, ST8 7JN

- o -

Library Association Besterman Medal, The

7 Ridgemont Street, London, WC1E 7AE

- o -

Library Association Carnegie Medal, The

7 Ridgemont Street, London, WC1E 7AE
- o -

Library Association Kate Greenaway Medal, The

7 Ridgemont Street, London, WC1E 7AE
- o -

Library Association McColvin Medal, The

7 Ridgemont Street, London, WC1E 7AE
- o -

Library Association Walford Award, The

7 Ridgemont Street, London, WC1E 7AE
- o -

Library Association Wheatley Medal, The

7 Ridgemont Street, London, WC1E 7AE
- o -

London Arts Board Publishing Fund

Elme House, 133 Long Acre, London, WC2E 9AF

- o -

LWT Plays On Stage

The London Television Centre, Upper Ground, London, SE1 9LT

- o -

Macaulay Fellowship

70 Merrion Square, Dublin 2, Eire

- o -

Macmillan Prize For Children's Books, The

18-21 Cavaye Place, London, SW10 9PG

- o -

Marsh Christian Trust Award

Authors' Club, 40 Dover Street, London, W1X 3RB

- o -

Martin Luther King Memorial Prize

7 Fore Street, Chard, Somerset, TA20 1PJ
- o -

Martin Toonder Award

An Chomhairle Ealaion, 70 Merrion Square,
Dublin 2, Republic of Ireland
- o -

Mathew Pritchard Award For Short Story Writing, The

95 Clyn Avenue, Lakeside, Cardiff, South
Glamorgan, CF2 6EL
- o -

McColvin Medal, The

7 Ridgmount Street, London, WC1E 7AE
- o -

McVitie's Prize For Scottish Writers, The

Scottish Legal Building, 95 Bothwell Street,
Glasgow, Strathclyde, G2 7HY
- o -

Montagu Of Beaulieu Trophy, The

30 The Cravens, Smallfield, Surrey, RH6 9QS

- o -

Mother Goose Award

Whiteway Court, The Whiteway, Cirencester, Gloucestershire, GL7 7BA

- o -

NASEN Special Education Needs Award

The Publishers Association, 19 Bedford Square, The Publishers Association, 19 Bedford Square, London, WC1B 3HJ

- o -

National Poetry Competition

22 Betterton Street, London, WC2H 9BU

- o -

Natural World Book Of The Year Award

20 Upper Ground, London, SE1 9PF

- o -

NCR Book Award For Non-Fiction

NCR Ltd, 206 Marylebone Road, London NW1 6LY

- o -

New Writers Award

Romantic Novelists' Association, 5 St Agnes Gate, Wendover, Bucks HP22 6DP

- o -

Northern Short Story Competition

Littlewood Arc, Nanholme Mill, Shaw Wood Road, Todmorden, Lancashire, OL14 6DA

- o -

Nottinghamshire Children's Book Award

Education Library Service, Glaisdale Parkway, Nottingham, NG8 4GP

- o -

Observer National Children's Poetry Competition

The Observer, 8 St Andrew's Hill, London EC4V 5JA

- o -

Odd Fellows Social Concern Book Award

45 East Hill, London, SW18 2QZ

- o -

Oldman Prize, The

Aberdeen University Library, Queen Mother Library, Meston Walk, Aberdeen, Lothian, AB9 2UE

- o -

One Voice Monologue Competition

c/o Pro Forma, Box 29 Neath, West Glamorgan, SA11 1WL

- o -

OWG/COLA Awards For Excellence

PO Box 520, Bamber Bridge, Preston, Lancashire, PR5 8LF

- o -

Pan Macmillan School Library Award

18-21 Cavye Place, London, SW10 9PG

- o -

PAWS Drama Script Fund, The

The PAWS Office, OMNI Communications,
Osbourne House, 111 Bartholomew Road,
London, NW5 2BJ

- o -

Pearson Television Theatre Writers' Society

Teddington Lock, Teddington, Middlesex, TW11 9NT

- o -

Peer Poetry Competition

26C Arlington House, Bath Street, Bath, BA1 1QN

- o -

Poetry Business Competition

The Studio, Byram Arcade, Westgate,
Huddersfield, West Yorkshire, 1HD1 1ND

- o -

Poetry Life Poetry Competition

14 Penington Oval, Lymington, Hampshire,
SO14 8BQ

- o -

Pro Dogs Open Creative Writing Competition

267 Hillbury Road, Warlington, Surrey, CR6 9TL

- o -

Prudence Farmer Award

Foundation House, 33 Kingsland Road, London,
E2 8DQ

- o -

Quaterfoil Award

Little Abington, Cambridge, CB1 6BQ

- o -

Radio Times Drama & Comedy Awards

35 Marylebone High Street, London, W1M 4AA

- o -

Regional Press Awards

Press Gazette, EMAP Business Communications, 33-39 Bowling Green Lane, London, EC1R 0DA

- o -

Renault UK Journalist Of The Year Award

Guild of Motoring Writers, 30 The Cravens, Smallfield, Surrey RH6 9QS

- o -

Rhone-Poulenc Prizes, The

COPUS c/o The Royal Society, 6 Carlton House Terrace, London, SW1Y 5AG

- o -

Rhys Davies European Travel Awards

3rd Floor, Mount Stuart House, Mount Stuart Square, Cardiff, CF1 6DQ

- o -

Richard Imison Memorial Prize, The

84 Drayton Gardens, London, SW10 9SB

- o -

Robinson Medal, The

7 Ridgmont Street, London, WC1E 7AE

- o -

Rogers Prize, The

University of London, Senate House, London, WC1E 7HU

- o -

Romantic Novelists Netta Muskett Award

9 Hillside Road, Southport, Merseyside PR8 4QB

- o -

Romantic Novelists Novel Of The Year

9 Hillside Road, Southport, Merseyside PR8 4QB
- o -

Romantic Novelists' Association Major Prize

3 Arnesby Lane, Peatling Magna, Leicester, Leicestershire, LE8 5UN
- o -

Romantic Novelists' Association New Writers Award

RNA Cobble Cottage, 129 New Street, Baddesley Ensor, Nr Atherstone, Warwickshire, CV9 2DL
- o -

Rose Mary Crawshay Prize, The

British Academy, 20-21 Cornwall Terrace, London NW1 4QP
- o -

Routledge Ancient History Prize

Richard Stoneman, Routledge, 11 New Fetter
Lane, London EC4P 1EE

- o -

Rover Group Award

Guild of Motoring Writers, 30 The Cravens,
Smallfield, Surrey, RH6 9QS

- o -

Royal Economic Society Prize, The

c/o University of York, York, North
Yorkshire, YO1 5DD

- o -

Royal Society Of Literature Award, The

Royal Society of Literature, 1 Hyde Park
Gardens, London W2 2LT

- o -

Royal Society Of Medicine Prizes, The

The Society of Authors, 84 Drayton Gardens,
London SW10 9SB

- o -

RTZ David Watt Memorial Award

6 St James's Square, London, SW1Y 4LD

- o -

Satire Society & Scotman Award, The

9 Fountain Close, 22 High Street, Edinburgh,
EH1 1TF

- o -

Schegel-Tieck Prize

84 Drayton Gardens, London, SW10 9SB

- o -

Science Book Prizes

6 Carlton House Terrace, London, SW1Y 5AG

- o -

Scott Moncrieff Prize

84 Drayton Gardens, London, SW10 9SB

- o -

Scottish Arts Council Book Awards

12 Manor Place, Edinburgh, Lothian, EH3 7DD

- o -

Scottish Arts Council Research Grants

Literature Dept, Scottish Arts Council, 12 Manor Place, Edinburgh EH3 7DD

- o -

Scottish Arts Council Writers' Bursaries

Literature Dept, Scottish Arts Council, 12 Manor Place, Edinburgh, EH3 7DD

- o -

Scottish International Open Poetry Competition, The

Ayrshire Writers & Artists Society, Irvine, Ayrshire KA11 3BW

- o -

SCSE Book Prize

Dept of Education Studies, University of Reading, Bulmershe Court, Reading, Berks RG6 1HY

- o -

Seebohm Trophy, The

Age Concern Book of the Year, 1268 London Road, London SW16 4ER

- o -

Signal Poetry Award

Lockwood, Station Road, South Woodchester, Stroud, Glos, GL5 5EQ

- o -

Silver PEN Non-Fiction Award

English Centre of PEN, 7 Dilke Street, London SW3 4JE

- o -

Sir Bannister Fletcher Prize Trust

Authors' Club, 40 Dover Street, London W1X 3RB

- o -

Sir Peter Kent Conservation Book Prize

45 East Hill, London, SW18 2QZ

- o -

Sir Roger Newdigate Prize

University of Oxford, University Offices, Wellington Square, Oxford OX1 2JD

- o -

Sir William Lyons Award

30 The Cravens, Smallfield, Surrey, RH6 9QS

- o -

Smith Corona Prize

3A High Street, Rickmansworth, Hertfordshire WD3 1HP

- o -

Somerset Maugham Trust Fund

84 Drayton Gardens, London, SW10 9SB

- o -

Sony Radio Awards

47-48 Chagford Street, London, NW1 6EB

- o -

Southern Arts Literature Award

13 St Clamants Street, Winchester,
Hampshire, SO23 9DQ

- o -

Southern Arts Literature Bursaries

13 Clements Street, Winchester, Hampshire,
SO23 9DQ.

- o -

Southern Arts Literature Prize

13 St Clement Street, Winchester,
Hampshire, SO23 9DQ

- o -

Southport Writers' Circle Poetry Competition

53 Richmond Road, Birkdale, Southport,
Merseyside PR8 4SB

- o -

Staple First Editions Project 97-98

Tor Cottage, 81 Cavendish Road, Matlock,
Derbyshire DE4 3HD

- o -

Steinbeck Award

William Heinemann Ltd, Michelin House, 81
Fulham Road, London SW3 6RB

- o -

Sunday Express Book Of The Year

Literary Editor, 245 Blackfrairs Road, London,
SE1 9UX

- o -

Sunday Times Award For Excellence In Writing, The

The Sunday Times, 1 Pennington Street,
London E1 9XW

- o -

Sunday Times Award For Small Publishers

Independent Publishers Guild, 25 Cambridge
Road, Hampton, Middlesex TW12 2JL

- o -

Sunday Times Small Publishers Competition

45 East Hill, London, SW18 2QZ

- o -

T E Utley Memorial Fund Award

38 Aldridge Road Villas, London, W11 1BR

- o -

Teixeira Gomes Prize, The

The Translators Association, 84 Drayton
Gardens, London SW10 9SB

- o -

TES Information Book Awards

Priory House, St John's Wood, London, EC1M 4BX

- o -

Time-Life Silver Pen Award

7 Dike Street, London, SW3 4JE

- o -

UEA Writing Fellowship

University of East Anglia, University Plain, Norwich Norfolk, NR4 7TJ

- o -

Unicorn Arts Theatre National Competition

Unicorn Theatre for Children, Arts Theatre, Great Newport Street, London WC2H 7JB

- o -

Vauxhall Trophy

Guild of Motoring Writers, 30 The Cravens, Smallfield, Surrey RH6 9QS

- o -

Vogue Talent Contest

Vogue House, Hanover Square, London W1R 0AD

- o -

Vondel Translation Prize, The

The Translators Association, 84 Drayton Gardens, London SW10 9SB

- o -

W H Smith Illustration Awards

45 East Hill, London, SW18 2QZ

- o -

W H Smith Literary Award

7 Holbein Place, London, SW1W 8NR

- o -

W H Smith Mind Boggling Books Award

Scope Communications, Tower House, 8-14 Southampton Street, London WC2E 7HA

- o -

W H Smith Plays For Children Awards

Quarry Hill Mount, Leeds, West Yorkshire, LS9 8AW

- o -

W H Smith Thumping Good Read Award

Scope Communications, Tower House, 8-14 Southampton Street, London WC2E 7HA

- o -

W H Smith Young Writers' Competition

7 Holbein Place, London, SW1W 8NR

- o -

Wadsworth Prize For Business History

Business Archives Council, The Clove Building, 4 Maguire Street, London SE1 2NQ

- o -

Wandsworth London Writers Competition

Room 224, Town Hall, Wandsworth High Street, London SW18 2PU

- o -

Welsh Arts Council Book Of The Year Award

Museum Place, Cardiff, CF1 3NX
- o -

West Midlands Arts Work & Production

82 Granville Street, Birmingham, West Midlands, B1 2LH
- o -

Wheatley Medal, The

7 Ridgmount Street, London, WC1E 7AE
- o -

Whitbread Book Of The Year

272 Vauxhall Bridge Road, London, SW1V 1BA
- o -

Winifred Mary Stanford Prize, The

47 Bedford Square, London, WC1B 3DP
- o -

WJM MacKenzie Prize, The

Dept of Politics & Comp History, University of Salford, Salford, M5 4WT

- o -

Wolfson History Prizes

18-22 The Haymarket, London, SW1Y 4DQ

- o -

Woolwich Young Radio Playwrights Competition

Independent Radio Drama Ltd, PO Box 518, Manningtree, Essex CO11 1XD

- o -

Writers Guild Awards, The

430 Edgeware Road, London W2 1EH

- o -

Yorkshire Post Author Of The Year

Yorkshire Post, PO Box 168, Wellington Street, Leeds, West Yorkshire LS1 1RF

- o -